This book can very
Beginners and top sales achievers alike
less lessons that are shared in this book. A lifetime of practical sales advice can be acquired within a few hours by reading *It's Your Deal.*

MAGNUS SUBLETT, REGIONAL OWNER AND DIRECTOR
REMAX INC.

Joe Sowerby offers practical, common sense advice for salespeople who are always looking to sharpen their game. He offers useful pointers for novices and gentle reminders for seasoned pros. Readers will be sold.

JOHN PEPPER, BUSINESS EDITOR
DETROIT NEWS

Recognizing the arduous demands of salesmanship, *It's Your Deal* is an excellent tool to build the mental and emotional stamina necessary for a career in sales. It is a positive guide for the young person just exploring the working world. It also serves as a clear refresher for the experienced.

JOSEPH D. REID, CHAIRMAN & CEO
CAPITOL BANCORP LTD.

It's Your Deal offers practical advice in short, to-the-point chapters. Sowerby's sales experience affords plenty of first-person anecdotes to support his points on everything from specific sales techniques to observations on ethics and keeping a balance between *living* and *working for a living*.

MARY KRAMER, ASSOCIATE PUBLISHER
CRAIN'S DETROIT BUSINESS

If you are tied in any way to the business world, this book will serve as a supercharged potion for your sense of ambition and meeting goals.

LARRY SMITH, PRESIDENT
AUTOMETRIC CORPORATION

Sowerby's book is a clear and real recipe for business and personal success. This 'chef' doesn't use, or need, fancy ingredients or an extravagant menu. But at the end you'll know you had a great meal, and you will know how to make your own. Readers will find themselves breezing through this entertaining and insightful book.

RON KAGAN, DIRECTOR
DETROIT ZOOLOGICAL INSTITUTE

The word 'salesperson' has lost its meaning in today's world because so few do what it takes to be successful. *It's Your Deal* is a real world guide for those committed to being *real* salespeople.

KEVIN C. RINKE, PRESIDENT
RINKE CADILLAC, RINKE TOYOTA AND RINKE PONTIAC,
THE #2 PONTIAC DEALER IN THE UNITED STATES

It's Your Deal brings a no nonsense, no excuse approach to making your life and career a success!

SARAH SERRA, VICE PRESIDENT & DIRECTOR
UNIVERSITY OF PHOENIX
MICHIGAN CAMPUS

Joe Sowerby presents uncommon wisdom about life through vignettes that will resonate with every reader. His user-friendly style belies the powerful core values of life presented in *It's Your Deal.* This is a must read for anyone wanting to live life fully.

GARY W. TISCORNIA, EXECUTIVE DIRECTOR
MICHIGAN HUMANE SOCIETY

A warm and friendly motivational book. It's like getting advice from your parents about how to be successful, the importance of helping others and even about your health, because the author really cares.

SUE MARX, ACADEMY AWARD WINNER

Joe Sowerby's book puts a fresh, creative face on getting up and going to work in the morning. This thought-provoking, stimulating, treatise reinforces what we are doing right and encourages us to explore new territory for a more mentally and emotionally compelling experience.

SANDY HERMANOFF, APR, FELLOW PRSA
CEO/PRESIDENT, HERMANOFF & ASSOCIATES

This book deals with universal truths about the sales profession. I would recommend it to all. Chapter Three was my favorite. I have seen whiners in every sales organization. They can be a cancer if left untreated, and every sales professional needs to be aware of them.

MICHAEL J. BEGLEY
MASSMUTUAL, THE BLUE CHIP COMPANY
MICHIGAN-BEGLEY ORGANIZATION

Joe Sowerby clearly defines the word 'flexible' (readily adjustable to changing conditions) and how the word relates to success. With his straightforward, honest approach to life's opportunities, he is ready to adjust, to modify his actions and to reach his goals. Credible advice from an expert, Sowerby's words are important reading for everyone in business.

ANGIE BOURNIAS, PRESIDENT
CREATIVE SERVICES

Great book, great job.

ANDREW MUMA, BOARD OF DIRECTORS
MICHIGAN ASSOCIATION OF INSURANCE AGENTS

It's Your Deal is a book with a mission. Light-hearted but serious, fast paced, humorous at times, and well worth the journey.

K. NOREEN KEATING, PRESIDENT, LIGHTHOUSE INC.
376 POINTS OF LIGHT AWARD RECIPIENT
FROM PRESIDENT GEORGE BUSH

Life is a Mission:

The successful marketing of our product
is the business side of that mission.

Service, determination, time well spent, honor
and integrity assure the success of our cause.

It's
YOUR DEAL

A REAL WORLD GUIDE TO SELLING WELL AND *Sleeping Well*

JOSEPH SOWERBY

Sage Creek Press

Traverse City, Michigan

Published by SAGE CREEK PRESS
121 E. Front Street, 4th Floor
Traverse City, Michigan 49684

Publisher's Cataloging-in-Publication Data
Sowerby, Joseph.
It's your deal: a real world guide to selling well and sleeping well / Joseph Sowerby. -- Traverse City, Mich.: Sage Creek Press, 1998.
p. ill. cm.
Includes bibliographical references and index.
ISBN 1-890394-21-1
1. Selling. I. Title.
HF5438.25 .S69 1998 98-85080
658.85 dc—21 CIP

Illustrations by Peter M. Richard
Cover design by Barbara Hodge

PROJECT COORDINATION BY JENKINS GROUP, INC.

02 01 00 99 ◆ 5 4 3 2 1

Printed in the United States of America

To my father
who knew I could.
And to my mother
who prayed that I would.

Contents

Foreword

When Joe Sowerby asked me to write this foreword I was flattered but surprised. I've only known Joe four years, since the day he came into our company. He has many colleagues of much-longer standing who will vouch both for him and for the large chunks of wisdom in this little book.

But after pondering Joe's request, I think I understood why he asked me instead of someone else. Joe joined this firm after being terminated from another job — something he didn't protest my mentioning here, and more important something that didn't slow him down for five minutes.

From Joe's perspective, his previous employer made a massive and grossly unfair mistake. It takes a true pro (most secrets of which are in this book) to do what Joe did. Instead of sitting on his baggage and watching the world go by, he went straight out and found another challenge. His gain, my gain. Joe quickly became our top producer.

Over the years I have had hundreds of employees, but I can't recall anyone with more determination. Joe is a motivated man who makes plans, sets goals and keeps an honest score. He practices what he preaches, and never quits preaching what he practices.

I have no doubt Joe will achieve whatever he sets out to do. Unlike many ambitious men, he maintains his integrity in his dealings, character in his behavior, and compassion for others — human beings and his beloved animals.

In this book, Joe writes of both his successes and his failures and what he has learned from both. He writes in hopes that you will benefit from his own experience.

I should have read this book 50 years ago — except Joe wasn't around to write it.

GEBRAN "GABE" S. ANTON
FOUNDER OF ANTON'S MENSWEAR
BOARD OF DIRECTORS CHATEAU ESTATES
PRESIDENT ANTON ZORN & ASSOCIATES REAL ESTATE

Introduction

"To be or not to be?"
A pretty easy choice.

As I debated whether to write this book, some questions held me back: "Am I really good enough? Do I have enough to say? Is what I say correct, important, accurate? GOOD ENOUGH?" Sound familiar? Do you see a familiar picture? Unless you're an out-of-control egomaniac, it is only natural to question ourselves this way.

The good news is that, yes, we are good enough. Each of us has a private story we have been writing for years, perhaps not with paper and pen but always with actions and deeds. It may be God's canvas and paint, but it's our deeds and actions that create the brush strokes and add color to the portrait that is our life and career.

Our mind is like a gun firing continuous tracer rounds in the form of thoughts. Don't ignore them or sentence them to unrealized oblivion.

It has been said, in many ways and often: you are you.

As much as you wish to connect with someone else, relate to someone else, sometimes even be someone else, the end result is that this is your skin, your life and your chunk of the universe. It really is your universe. It was not created by us, but the piece of it we inhabit is ours — from our nose to our toes and most especially from the eyebrows up. Our design is whatever we choose — comfort, speed, cruising, just staying still. The choice is ours. The design, the course of our lives belongs to us.

This is not to say that outside influences, those around us and close to us, don't take part in the molding and shaping. In the end, however, we are the first face we see in the mirror in the morning and the last face in the mirror at night. That unknown committee of they — all the "theys" in our life who have a bearing in our life, for better or worse — are not there unless we allow them to be, an imaginary parrot on our shoulders. You are worthy — I am worthy — grab hold of that fact and don't let go.

Sometimes life may seem like a great big leering toilet bowl and there we are, hanging on to the edge while life's problems, heartaches and challenges take turns trying to flush us down. Hang on — never let go. You might break a nail or an arm. You might break your heart. Don't let go — when the toilet is through flushing, the clean, pure water of life always reappears. No matter how many times fate and your adversaries flick that handle.

Acknowledgments

Life has blessed me with role models, mentors and the gift of being able to recognize them. To those of you who believed, taught, praised, pushed, coaxed, gave me a break or delivered that swift kick in the nick of time, thank you.

It's your deal, too!

Special appreciation to my editor, Tom Ferguson, for his literary wisdom; and to Katayoon, you're the best.

One

Is It A Career Or Just A Place To Go?

Don't tiptoe around.
Come in for a committed landing.
It's not empty words, but effort, that keeps us outstanding.

In over two decades as a salesman I have crossed paths with many competent, diligent colleagues — a far larger percentage than the public gives us credit for. Many of the not-so-diligent — in sales or elsewhere in the work force — think they are on the way to something else.

They're like a high school student holding down a co-op job. "Once I grow up and decide what to do, I'll quit car sales, appliance sales, clothing sales — whatever kind of sales — and get a real job," they say. "Some time

I'll stop fooling around with real estate commission sales and go 9-to-5 with a salary."

The main drawback to this thought is that you aren't just killing time, you're assassinating it, along with real opportunities for success. This mode of thought allows you to be less than committed while going through the motions. The problem is that much of life is a race to be run and five, ten or fifteen years can pass while you're deciding what you want to be.

We justify the waste with the time-honored reasoning of "I've got a job, I'm not collecting unemployment, I'm supporting my family, etc., etc." Meanwhile, the race is being run all around us and we're still loosening up at the starting line.

I've got news for you, the starting gun is in our hands and no one else's — not our parents, spouses or employers. Our finger is on the trigger of our career, but you can't win if you don't play, and you're not playing if you're just going through the motions. Any salespeople out there who are just waiting for something better to drop into your lives, those of you waiting for that "REAL JOB", you know who you are. Get a grip — you've got the best job there is. A company can design a product, think it, produce it, display it. Without salespeople to take it to the public, it rarely makes a ripple. Without that elusive middle-man quality, that ability, that instinct and determination to succeed, kick-started by goals and income, scores of thousands of great ideas and concepts by thinkers who are not marketers and deal-closers would never hit the retail shelf.

The best thing about the sales profession is no one can take it away from you! Don't mumble at a party when people ask what you do. "I'm in sales." Stick out your chest and announce it. People get laid off or fired from a one-track career; some go to college four or six years to learn one job and find no openings in the field. What happens to an engineer or patternmaker in a saturated market? What are they going to do? In sales, your field is anything marketable. Job availability is endless. This is not to suggest you bounce around selling everything. It is good, and professional, to find your niche. But the possibilities are endless. Flexibility is a reality, not a concept, in sales. We are blessed to be able to do what we do.

I've heard several speakers use the analogy of breakfast foods to illustrate commitment to one's position in life, be it job, marriage, a relationship, whatever. The next time you're eating breakfast, think of the difference between the chicken and the pig. Oh yes, the chicken is involved, she laid the eggs, good, fresh and tasty. But if you want to look for the real commitment, then look no further than the pig on your plate. That pig is committed. Are you merely involved with your career, or committed to the full-bore results that are possible?

Don't circle the airport of life looking for a soft spot to land. There are none. We make our own soft spots

I'll find a place to land one of these years.

through effort and commitment. If we circle that airport too long, we run out of gas. Life is full of choices, so make one.

If you choose sales, that's only a start. Choose to commit yourself to a job well done, and the job will do well by you. Choose to coast and drift, and you are looking at a crash.

Two

Just One Person

You are the marker
in the game of life play.
One is the number
so get on with your day.

Failing is easy, if that is where our comfort zone is. I don't intend to judge or demean. I've failed plenty at lots of different things. I can suggest this — the difference between success and failure can be microscopic. Worse yet, both can be inaccurate perceptions, as different as a relaxing afternoon nap and a pit bull attaching itself to your ankle. It all boils down to acceptance — not surrender, acceptance.

Human nature makes us guard what we perceive as ours. Are you protecting your negative feelings, hoarding them like precious stones because they belong to you, putting them in the same emotional dresser drawer as the positive aspects of your life? It's like getting dressed in the dark — you wind up with one brown sock and one blue sock and fail to notice the difference. Do it long enough and you rob yourself of the attitude, strength and courage it takes to see the difference.

Life is a deal. Your job is bad, your marriage is great, so you deal with it. Your love life stinks, business is great, you deal with it. Hear the sound of running water? The toilet is flushing one part of your life. The bowl is filling up with fresh water in another part. This might be a tough question, a trick question...but what should you focus on? The tainted water being flushed or the fresh water coming in? Gain strength from the fresh water to deal with the foul. Don't taint the fresh water with the negative past of the foul. The toilet is running. Which commode are you running to — fresh or foul?

Help has many disguises, features and — mostly — benefits. Help is always on the way. Why? Because we are always on our way through life, and life is set up in such a way that it is user-answer-friendly. If you use life — break it in like a well-oiled baseball glove, or the soft rich soil of a fertile flower bed — then things get caught, things grow a lot better.

Absorb what you see and hear; don't deflect it. Take solace from failure — you have learned and you'll try to remember. In equal doses, learn and forget. Forget the negative results of a deal. Learn why the results were what they were, absorb the lesson, not the negative feeling. You might say those negative feelings motivate me. Motivation is one thing, letting them eat you alive, chew you up and spit you out is another. Thoughtful, deliberate observation, in a sales situation, sharpened with the desire for success, is always better than venom and anger in achieving a goal.

I call the latter vindictive sales, sales with an attitude. That last customer was rude and wasted your time, so the next customer becomes a victim instead of a client because of your anger. No one owes you a deal. You put a stinky attitude out to the public and you'll get a stinky response. No one owes you anything. We do owe ourselves and our time the best we can offer. A bad moment, a bad day, can happen. Nobody's perfect, but get over it and move on. Perhaps what Satchel Paige was referring to when he uttered those immortal words, "Don't look back, something might be gaining on you," was as much about attitude and spirit as some imaginary bogeyman.

Joe Delaney was just one man and his true greatness makes me pause. He was a rising star in the National Football League, gifted running back for the Kansas City Chiefs. His last words were, "I don't swim so good, but I've got to do something." With those words, he leaped into deep water trying to save a drowning child. Neither one made it.

Delaney was on top of the world and he put it all in

harm's way to save another human, knowing he didn't swim well. He was just one person, and one of my heroes. I never met the man, but he must have had an attitude of trying to make a difference. Sure we are just one person, but every day — many times a day — we have smaller opportunities and easier choices that will make a difference. For ourselves and for others.

Three

Keeping Smoke Out Of Your Eye

You are your own best shot.
Locked, loaded and ready to fire.
Avoid overgrown babies and back stabbers who would have you be less than what you are.

Beware of whiners. In so many work situations, commission sales or otherwise, there is always a whiner. They are attitude anchors in a swimming pool, trying to attach themselves to your ankle at the deep end. These human anchors can be harmful to your future and certainly to your financial well being.

A bad attitude anchor is like kissing someone with a runny nose. You both end up with a cold. Bad attitudes will hold you back, hold you down and color your entire business acumen in a dull shade of gray — hardly a way to get ahead. Attitudes happen. Let it happen to someone else, if need be. Let it go and let it flow.

If the attitude barracuda bites you on the leg, bandage it up, take an attitude antidote and get on with the show. Does it make much sense to stick your leg in a pool with a hungry barracuda, and after you get bit, leave it there so that it can get a second course? Spear that barracuda, don't give in to prolonged woe-is-me attitudes on the job. What you are liable to find is that "woe is me" with a job is nothing compared to "woe is me" without a job, when your employer or boss gets tired of the complaining and whining and decides replacing you is the solution.

I have found in sales that it's easy to identify the whiners — the anchor attitude people trying to drag me or others into the mud and murk of a crummy mood. For someone with a bad attitude in the workplace, every day is Christmas and they want to pass out gifts of guilt, remorse, failure, recrimination and second-guessing. Don't open that package.

The most insidious whiner is the successful whiner. He has been at the same job for years, makes a good income and has watched the rookies and others come and go. Have you ever gone to work somewhere and the old pro is always holding court, always ready to tell you what's wrong with the operation? They could do more business if they would do this differently or do that dif-

And another thing I don't like about this place ...

ferently, if their advertising didn't stink, if the sales manager was stronger, if service was better, if only they would have taken on that new product line. Why allow someone to cause you worry and grief over things you can't control? Remember the expression, "Worry is the interest paid on things that never happen."

Often the successful whiner gets everyone else looking for the potholes in the road, when in reality there are none, or they can easily be patched. However, because the whiner is the old dog, the old pro, you listen and the smoke gets so thick you can't tell the forest from the trees. You know the old saying, "If you look hard enough for a problem you'll find one or two or three." That's a killer whether you're new on a job, or trying to maximize your potential as an old dog without an attitude.

By the way, the old professional whiner goes about his business, makes a couple of deals or more, despite the poor working conditions he's been warning you about. So while you're worrying about what might be wrong, he's depositing checks.

Something else I've found out about seasoned whiners is that they rarely lobby for change. Most whiners are under-the-breath complainers, spineless to the workplace and their employer. They will hypocritically, secretly revel in bringing you down with their poisonous pep rallies. They are not your allies. Success respects your attendance — failure loves it.

The other common type of whiner is, well, more common. They are average or less. They are not as talented and insidious as the successful whiner. If they were, they would have been smart enough to change their attitude and move up or move on, or at least not let the successful whiner poison them and make a lower, mid-level whiner out of them. In large organizations there is a pecking order, even among whiners.

The mid-level whiner doesn't have enough guts to change for the better and move on, up or out of the way. They worry about not being last or at best being a good solid drone bee in the organization. They're usually not as vocal as the successful whiner. When they are, it's especially pathetic.

Both types emit a low growl that dissolves into a whine about how things are and how they should be. If they had to do it over they wouldn't be here, but every day is a chance to do it over — and here they are. What does that tell you? Mostly it's the jelly in their spines that gives them away. They are opinionated enough to try to slow you down, hold you back and make you question your own worth, but when push comes to shove and it's time for them to stand up for the "changes" they demand, to be strong and be counted, they melt into the pavement. They have to go to the restroom or pick up lunch. Then they resurface like a case of bad gas at the moment they sense an opportunity to complain.

The only things we control on this planet are how we think and how we feel. Never surrender or compromise that privilege by allowing others in life, especially the workplace, to bring us down.

These smoke-screen specialists can rarely be counted on, so count them out. If anyone is to influence us, let it be the winners, not the whiners.

Four

Follow-Up: From A Ripple To A Wave

Toll booths of effort
keep the roof over our head.

Your business may start out small, but if you continuously follow up and keep a file of prospects, you go from being a pebble in a big lake to a brick tossed into a small pond. You create impact. Following up creates credibility. It shows prospects and clients that you're serious. Equally important, it proves to you that you're serious and committed. If you look committed, act committed and think committed, you are committed. Walk like a duck, talk like a duck...you're a duck.

Large or small, it's your business, your turf. Treat

your prospects like they're valued customers and they will be customers. That's not to say that you're going to win everyone over. Be it life or sales, you will never win everyone over. That does not translate into giving up. Analyze why you could or couldn't, but never give up.

Personal chemistry is a real thing. Sometimes people don't click. Sometimes deals just weren't designed to be made between two people. Let me say this — there is no worse feeling for the insightful salesperson than to know that a deal failed because of something he or she neglected to cover. That's not to say that you beat yourself up for the next six months, six weeks or six days. That is to say, live and learn — and learn, and learn.

And remember. While you live and learn and learn and learn, follow up, follow up, follow up. There are plenty of competent follow-up systems available. I'll spend time introducing the one that works for me. It is basic, creates depth in your daily schedule and is highly mobile. However the critical thing is to *do* it. Be consistent, be steady and do it. Politely, professionally, follow up. Then follow up some more.

I've heard it said so many times in so many ways that people waste time, kill time and ignore the value of time at work. It's a poor state of affairs if you're a slacker punching a clock; it's wrong as a commission salesperson hanging out at the water cooler. The difference is, on a clock you shortchange your employer and yourself. As a salesperson, you cheat yourself, your employer, yourself, your opportunity, yourself, your family --- see the picture? Sales is an opportunity. No one can take our ability and opportunities away from us better than ourselves. On a clock, your pay is your pay, sometimes commensurate with your worth, sometimes not. Commission sales compensation is almost always equal to effort.

Provided your employer is not holding you back, sales is a reflection of what your time is worth. Your employer can hold you back with poor pay plans, poor working conditions, no advertising and a bad environment. Sometimes that lament is legitimate; however, how many times have you heard someone complaining about all kinds of real or imagined circumstances that are holding them back while the person one office over just hums along, never saying a word and depositing large checks? Attitude usually determines altitude.

If you follow up, follow up, follow up — with a plan, the opportunities will always be more plentiful. Even without a plan, follow up enhances results. Throw enough stuff against the wall, something will stick.

Are you planning for success, or planning your excuses? It's never my fault. My car broke down. My spouse doesn't understand. If only we had more inventory. If only we had different inventory. This is a rotten place to work, my boss is terrible, if only we had less inventory, a better location, a better pay plan. Got about five years — I can keep on going.

How about a kinder, gentler world that hands out

kudos and paychecks — regardless of performance? Sounds less like a solution than a fairy tale by the Brothers Grimm, in which the wicked attitude witch and the fire-breathing dragon took your paycheck.

Quite often the negative attitude that we perceive in our place of employment starts in our own head and ends in our heart. Where we stand mentally and emotionally from a professional standpoint in those two places — more than any outside force we perceive, real or imaginary — will either keep us from where we want to be, or take us to newfound heights.

Five

Your Job Should Be A Friend

It's your buddy, pal, chum.
Get a good grip.
Hold on tight. It's yours to keep or give away.

A job can be your escape, your ally, a pair of sneakers you depend on. A really good job, well done, can be your closest friend. Your relationship with what you do for financial livelihood should never be less than a friendly, nodding acquaintance.

If you have regressed to a sullen, dispirited relationship with "what you do," then give real consideration to moving on. Of course, if the reason for the sour relationship is that everything in your life is that way, then forget this chapter. Stop here and go buy *Feeling Good,*

The New Mood Therapy, by David Byrne. It is a thought-provoking book that worked for me.

Really folks, if what you do for a living is spiteful, nasty, demeaning, lessens you as a person or you just can't stand it, start looking around. Fill out some job applications and pass out resumés. Remember one important thing — do not, I repeat, do not, do not, do not quit unless you have another position lined up. It is always better and easier to find a job while you've got a job. Mentally it's better; you're not pressing as hard. You may not like where you are at but it does pay. You look far better to a potential employer if rather than needing a job, you're looking for a job.

The great thing about making plans is that you can change them. It's tough to unwind your plans once you've put them into action, so think about your actions as much as you think about your plans.

What we do for a living represents a huge chunk of our lives, work toward enjoying your job. If you can relish it, great; but if you hate it, how good are you going to be? How far are you going to go? Countless speakers, authors and leaders have said that attitude determines altitude. If you are unhappy with what you are doing, you are like a loaded 747 trying to get off the runway on one engine.

Nowhere is this more critical than in a position that deals with the public. Except in a position that must sell to the public. Attitude can make you or break you the quickest of all. Employers beware too — the trickle-down effect is a living, breathing thing, not just an economic theory. What you do by your employees, through your employees, for your employees, with your employees, will make or break their job friendship. Create a mean, intimidating atmosphere at your workplace and you might get short-term results, but seldom will you get the warm, deep satisfaction of a long-term shared relationship with success.

The give and take of the workplace is a powerful tool for all. Being wanted and appreciated, along with genuine concern by employer and employee, coupled with a few sound ideas that are put into action, is seldom a formula that leads to anything but success.

Six

Meeting And Greeting

Smile big.
"Hello." "Good morning." "Good afternoon."
"Thanks for stopping in."
A good start makes for a strong finish.

It all sounds so simple, and in many ways it is. Our first impression — our opening sentences, statements and reactions in a sales introduction — are often the barometer for future results. What you say, how you say it, the way it is measured and received can, many miles later, be the deal maker.

We are on the job. Meeting and greeting the public is part of our position. Our pay is generally commensurate with our success. Doesn't it make sense to put your best foot forward all the time, even with the least likely prospect? Is a smile, a bright greeting and an open mind too much to ask of ourselves? You might ask what I mean by an open mind. It means the ability to start every day and every fresh sales situation with the opinion that a deal can be made anew, not lost again. It also means don't pre-qualify customers.

It starts with the first "Hello," be it in person, on the phone, even via the Internet. Basics, basics, basics. Football players, baseball players and every other athlete has training camp. Sales is no different. In the business of sales, training camp is every day. Every day we're at the arena of our employment, we decide the level of our game.

A strong greeting is essential. By strong I don't necessarily mean a loud, "Yahoo, howdy partner" or an attempt to overwhelm in the first thirty seconds. Everyone should develop his or her own style, one that is comfortable. The point is to have a style, to be consistent, to give an air of warmth and comfort. Being in charge of the conversation or directing the dialogue does not mean taking over the conversation.

Attitude controls conversation. If you approach a person with a warm greeting, delivered in a positive, friendly tone, the conversation will most likely continue in that tone. Immediately you are thinking about a rude person or unpleasant experience where you were pleasant and informative, but the customer was still rude and nasty. So what? Are you going to allow someone who is rude and negative to influence your behavior toward others in a manner that will make you less effective? Most people are nice. Let them set the example for our behavior.

It is important to become comfortable with a pleasant, effective, generic greeting. It's even better to have several and make an effort to improve upon them. It keeps us sharper.

Here are a few greetings I have used over the years: "Good morning (or afternoon), how may I assist you?" "Hello, thanks for stopping in. How may I help you?" "Welcome to XYZ Company. How may I help (or assist) you?" "Thanks for coming in on this beautiful day (or cold day or rainy day). How may I help?"

Nothing is more effective than sincere appreciation. Any greeting is better when positive vocal tones, open body language and a "thank you" are included in the greeting. Some salespeople open their greeting with an introduction. I'm not comfortable doing this. Often consumers in sales situations are nervous, feel pressured just being there and are defensive about giving out their name in their first breath to a stranger.

A better strategy is to spend a few calculated moments gaining rapport and a friendly atmosphere. At that time a simple, "Oh, by the way, my name is Joe and your name is ...?" accomplishes the same thing with less risk of putting a person ill at ease or under pressure.

Many times when we greet someone, the first thing out of their mouth is, "Just looking," or the equivalent. It is important not to let your approach get derailed or stalled at that point. Have a pleasant, non-threatening, snappy response to, "I'm just looking."

The responses I have used with the most success are, "That's where it all begins" and "That's how it all starts." Some others are: "Did you have anything in particular in mind?" or "I may be able to save you some time. Did you have something in mind?" Put a big smile on your face and say, "Fantastic, may I help you look?" or "Great, did you have a particular style in mind?"

Be prepared to keep the conversation flowing. The profession of sales is about communication and keeping those lines of communication open. We have twice as many ears as tongues for a reason. Once the lines of communication are open, be sure to listen to what's being said.

In a good greeting, what you say and how you say it are equally important. You may have a great message, but if you deliver it like your dog just died, the message loses its meaning. On the other hand, you can be friendly and enthusiastic; but if all you are delivering is mindless drivel, people will see through you.

An effective greeting gets the ball rolling, puts other people at ease and also helps put us at ease. A good greeting and introduction creates sales impetus, rapport and common ground. Keep it fresh, friendly and appreciative. A good opening kick-off gives us a strong starting field position.

Seven

Look The Part

A clean car always runs better.

A brief note on your work wardrobe. Don't dress to test. Wear what is appropriate. If your employment environment is dressy casual, look the part. If it's suit and tie, the same applies. Dress for success is an old adage that always has applied, and always will.

When you choose your wardrobe for the day, assume you are going to be involved in an important event. After all, your career is an important event.

I remember coming to work one Friday in a rather dressed-down manner. There was nothing special on my schedule for the day. That morning I received a referral from a large bank. It was an important client of theirs who had a large building to sell. He wanted to see me that day; in fact, he was leaving town and had to see me within the hour.

He greeted me in a suit and tie. I was in a sport shirt and casual slacks. I was very uncomfortable. It was a large deal and I was not dressed in a manner that was appropriate. I apologized for my dress and he overlooked it — I'm sure in large part because of the fact that the bank had preordained me. The next time I might not be so lucky.

Have pride in your appearance. Don't go to work rumpled and unkempt. A sideways crease in your pants where they have been resting on a hanger, or the accordion effect that will develop at the top of a pair of slacks from wearing them too often with no dry cleaning or iron touch-up, will not cut it.

If your income is limited and your wardrobe reflects that, so be it. Just take what you have and look sharp. A $100 outfit or a $500 outfit both look the same if your shirt is wrinkled, your tie has gravy stains and it looks like you slept in your suit coat.

A sharp shirt and accessories with polished shoes does wonders for an inexpensive suit. An ill-fitting, wrinkled shirt, mismatched colors and scuffed shoes will make an expensive suit look like twenty-five cents.

The way you dress shows the level of respect you have for the two most important people in your career - yourself and your customers.

Eight

Form Follows Function: Consistent Persistence

It's our gift to ourselves day after day.
So render unto Caesar what is Caesar's
and make commission pay.

It's been described a thousand ways. All flash and no cash, lots of show and no dough, all looks and no heart, a hand full of gimme and a mouth full of much obliged. There are many apt descriptions. What it boils down to is that you can look the part and act the part, but you're beating an empty tin can if you fail to put forth the effort to be the part.

I continually use the term "follow-up," with good reason. Follow-up overcomes the mighty, overcomes the competition, and, given a good system and consistency,

A science to selling — you mean we have to do more than just show up?

follow up even overcomes our own shortcomings, misgivings and mistakes. In sales, sometimes we earn our money and get paid, earn our money and don't get paid or get paid for barely earning our money. It all evens out. Persistence and determination are the genies in the bottle, the difference in the formula — the formula being the 80/20 rule, that 20 percent of the salespeople make 80 percent of the sales. Develop an urgency to do business, a controlled fire in your belly, and you'll be among the 20 percent.

Keep in touch with your customers, clients, people — however you choose to think of them. Take the possessive positive: they're yours. In sales, your customers are the brick and mortar that builds your business. Building a customer base is no different than building a house.

The footings come first. Work consistently. I didn't say constantly. I said consistently. All work and no play isn't fun, but success is! It allows time for play. I would go so far as to suggest success can make our work like play.

Results, not time spent, are what counts. Working long hours with no direction or consistent effort is far less efficient than getting in, getting to work and getting the job done. Whether it's two hours or twenty, it's not the time that counts, it's the effort and results.

When you close a deal, that customer should become your property and your responsibility, not just your own personal victory. Every time.

A customer is so often viewed as a liability, a possible adversary, a future headache. But customers now more than ever expect service and accountability. What's wrong with that? Problem solving presents opportunities that, when coupled with follow up, are an elixir that breeds success. Solve a problem and you create loyalty and trust. Follow up and you form a bond of mutual accountability. Not a bad foundation to start from. Your job, your ally, your friend.

Fresh sales and repeat sales are the trusses and girders

that continue the project. Treating your business like a business accelerates the structure toward completion, leaving the best yet to come.

Repeat business is a fantastic element to any business. The air of mutual accountability, trust and confidence creates a client-customer bond that should tickle any successful peddler. It should also make us thankful that we have the opportunity to work this hard, enjoy what we have, be successful, and in addition to all that, actually have people in our business life who look forward to seeing us, and who enjoy doing business with us. That is a wonderful place to be. Customers become friends, friends become customers. And we get paid!

Yes, I know someone is reading this and saying, "What about the disloyal client, how about the price gouger?" Learn from failures and don't become cynical. Forget them. Count your victories. Don't dwell on defeats, just understand why you lost and let them go. Hoard memories of success and you will become victorious again.

Now for the final step in the building process: Referrals. What fun, what a pleasure. But never forget they are a responsibility. Referrals give you built-in, preordained credibility when handled properly. I said they're fun, and they should be. Less tension, less testing, less qualifying — which should give the professional more time to concentrate on customer satisfaction and closing, the two ingredients that make a tasty sales stew.

A pleasure, you ask, dealing with an unpredictable public, one that asks a lot and often gives little? A good sales situation can become a reciprocally positive experience between you and your client. He receives product and service; you receive income and success.

Referrals are a responsibility. Never take a referral for granted. Note them and pay for them, if appropriate, and always acknowledge them with a phone call, whether successful or not.

Think about it. If you took your time, your credibility and in some cases your responsibility and referred someone's business to an associate — someone you know or in whom you have displayed confidence — and they don't come through, doesn't that hurt? I don't mean so much if they make the deal or not. Deals come and deals go. If you work hard, smart and persistently, they happen. A good effort usually prevails.

What I mean by responsibility is when the referral is not acted upon, the follow-up call is not made, courtesy is not extended in a professional manner and the bridge of credibility is broken for both the party getting the referral and, to a lesser degree, for the person who suggested that their friend see you to start with.

It can also have a negative impact on the existing client/salesperson relationship that led to the referral in the first place.

The key is to take every opportunity, large or small, to set yourself apart from the crowd and once you have done that, to follow through and be better than the crowd.

One of my favorite ways of staying in touch with clients when I sold cars was to send out humorous Thanksgiving cards. There are a lot of holiday cards flying around, but I haven't seen many Thanksgiving cards.

When we fail to take advantage of repeat business opportunities, when we fail to diligently follow up on referral business, we are failing to treat our business like a business — which violates the integrity of the structure we are building. In that case, golden opportunity is reduced to a house of cards.

Nine

Being In Charge Doesn't Mean Charging Over

Leave your spurs in your saddlebag.
Your soldiers need a break.
There is no glory in finding out
how much someone can take.

In charge and charging over — it's the difference between a rapid dog and a rabid dog. Bosses, managers, owners, acolytes of owners, beware. If you don't like spinach don't stuff it down someone else's throat.

Being in charge is a responsibility, a gift and a compliment. Treat it as such. If you base your success on the success of those who work for you, your position will be a lot easier.

Lead by example, not lip service. Do what you say and say what you do.

Here is an easy analogy for leadership. Lie an ink pen on the table and try to push it with your fingertip. After a short distance it curves, wavers and goes off course. Take the front of the same pen and pull it. That pen will follow you anywhere. Pushing, bullying and lip service have no staying power.

I am reminded of a story I was told about Mahatma Ghandi. A mother brought her son to see him in the hope he would tell her child to stop eating sugar. She made her request and Ghandi told her to return in 30 days. She did as requested and Ghandi told her son to stop eating sugar. The mother was puzzled. "Why," she asked, "did you have me come back after 30 days?" His reply was, "First I had to stop eating sugar."

Lead by example, say what you do and do what you say. If you tell the truth, you don't have to remember what you said. If your employees are expected to start at 8:30 a.m. then you arrive at 8:30 a.m. You want your staff to be polite then you must be polite. If you run a car lot and it's snowing, be the first one out with a broom in your hand to clean off cars. Lip service is transparent motivation, easily seen through and quickly smudged; a cheap window display that no one will buy into.

Bite Your Tongue

Go figure
Pulling the trigger
Announcing thoughts
That leave powder burns
Leave them unfired.
Better off in their chambers
And then
Check the twitch
On tomorrow's finger itch

Ten

Capture The Positive

A net,
a butterfly
and you.

Capture your positive thoughts, hang on to them like a palm tree grips the soil during a tropical storm. I don't mean that yahoo, Pollyanna kind of positive — although by all means if that's what works, use it.

What I do mean is the deep, strong feeling of right, that you know how it's done. You've been there, done that, and you know how to prevail and hang tough if the situation warrants it. Hang onto your strengths, don't let momentary circumstances cause you to waiver.

In my life I've been up and down, and I've been around a lot of other people who were up and down, fighting with their spouse, complaining about the kids, problems with the house, trouble at work — heck, any excuse will do. I've been around a lot of people I call a mood a minute types. They're up, they're down, up, down, up, down, up, down. Steady is better. A trip up and down the mood elevator of life once in awhile is okay for a temporary tweak. But a constant dose creates a serious case of motion sickness both for us and those with whom we have daily contact.

Eleven

Making Haste Slowly: Mechanics For Follow-Up

Be true to your school.
Follow-Up University is its name.
A rare opportunity indeed
to assure the outcome of the game.

Good intentions are nice; certainly they are better than bad intentions. However, good intentions without a direction, plan or follow-through are idle chatter.

I told you "follow-up" would be my mantra. Now I want to show you how. There are many methods of effective follow-up. In this section I will give you one that has worked for me with easy, basic efficiency since I was introduced to it a number of years ago. The system can be easily computerized if you are so inclined. I'm sure there are others equally as effective or more high-tech. But like most things in life, if you talk the talk but don't walk the walk, you're only putting a quarter tank of fuel in your success tank. The following walk is a proven one.

My method is basic, sound, and after working this system for awhile it becomes exciting. The tools for "The System" are these:

1. A large date calendar/appointment book for the year we are in.
2. One file box, either 3x5 or 4x6 size.
3. An alphabetical divider.
4. A monthly divider.
5. An ample supply of file cards to catalog our customers.

Note I used the possessive "our customers." That is what any good business does, it makes a customer "your customer." When you feel they are your customer and the client feels they are your customer, life becomes so much easier. I know it sounds basic and corny, but it's absolute, functional truth.

This is how the system is set up. We meet a prospective customer in person, by phone or by referral. It is important, without pressuring them, to gain information about them. What we are trying to do is start a personal index card on those we meet in our daily business affairs.

The more complete our profile of the customer, the better prepared we are to service his needs, gain his confidence and ultimately reach our goal of a successful transaction. Below please view a basic file card on a prospective customer.

Date:	Date
Name:	
Address:	
Home Phone:	
Work Phone:	
Type of product looking for:	
Personal info:	
Pertinent facts regarding follow-up details of visits or phone calls:	

The date in the left-hand corner is the date they came in to see you the first time or your first conversation with them. The date in the right-hand corner is the date you mailed them a brief thank-you note acknowledging their visit or phone call. Time permitting, the note should be on the same day as their call or visit. The dates are important as a point of personal reference. They help jog our memories about past conversations. The note is to establish your credibility and sincerity. It raises your posture and puts you above the crowd, provided you follow up on the image you are building. If you tell someone you are going to do something, then do it!

Name, address and phone numbers are self-explanatory. Don't trust your memory on what someone was looking for — write it down. It is self-defeating to go through the motions of follow up without information. It's great to head west following the sun, but you'll see the Pacific a lot sooner with a map. The more detail you can convey to a customer regarding their wants and needs and the better-informed and knowledgeable you are on the subject, the better-received your follow-up will be. A fumbling follow-up is better than none, but if you're going to start dinner, you might as well set the oven at the proper temperature.

The same notion applies to personal information about customers. I don't mean age, weight, religion or gender, although remembering those things is okay. What I am referring to are personal tidbits. Are they

10/15/98 (Date in)	10/15/98 (Date note mailed)
Ann Smith 2200 Cumberland Rose City, MI 48222 Office # 222-2222	Home # 322-4588
Looking for 4-door economy car	
Works at Sears, needs 4-door for volunteer work, broken ankle	

from the area? What type of work do they do? What is their family status? Did they come in on crutches? Did their conversation touch on other subjects besides our product — sports, politics, fashion etc? Note these items on your file card.

11/27/98	11/28/98
Bob Thomas 33 Caribou West Branch, MI 48202 Office # 828-9999	Home # 777-8888
Looking for 10,000 SF Industrial Bldg. on E side of town, owns a mfg. firm that makes wiglets	
Interested in Detroit Red Wings and sports in general	

The purpose of the notes is simple. You don't have to sound like a one-track robot when you follow up. Yes, you have a purpose in mind when you call. However, when you can soften your intention with sincere, friendly, ice-breaking dialogue, it helps considerably. How's your ankle healing? How is your job at Sears treating you? Have you been doing much volunteer driving lately? And, oh by the way, I have a car I'd like you to look at. That works a lot better than "Uh, hi, this is so and so, have you purchased a car yet? And by the way I just got a nice little coupe in on trade that I'd like you to see; oh, I forgot, you wanted a four-door."

Most small, personal facts can be gained by a casual

introductory conversation. The secret is to reduce it to note form on your index card while the conversation is still fresh in your mind. When I sold cars, if I failed to close the sale on their first visit, the customer was barely out the door and I would be back at my desk writing a brief letter thanking them for the visit and putting it in the mail, making out a file card with information and notes, and putting a note in my appointment book to call them the next day or whatever day I said I would call at the close of our meeting.

Then, when making a follow-up call or seeing them on our next appointment, I am no stranger to them; nor are they to me. Make notes on your file card of all subsequent phone calls and meetings, along with the dates on which they took place.

Some days your schedule will be full and you won't open your file once. However, on days with a lot of open time, the file is a great tool. Thumb through it in the morning and pull eight or ten names to call. Thumb through it again in the afternoon. Perhaps someone you failed to think about comes to mind, or maybe you're just feeling more energetic. As time goes on, the file grows. It will become large enough that it can take days to get through it.

If you take names and are consistent in the process we discuss in this chapter, your inventory of clients can't help but grow. The time you spend at your desk will go by not only faster because you're busy, but more profitably because you are being constructive with your time, treating your business like a business!

10/1/98	**10/1/98**
Customer	
Address	
Phone	
Notes, etc.	
10/3 Good follow-up call, friendly, still looking	
10/10 Made appointment to show five acres on 10/12	
10/12 Showed property, meeting with banker	

If you used the system effectively, each conversation will be an extension of the prior meeting or conversation. You will have less awkward silences in the ebb and flow of your conversation, which allows more mutual comfort. You become an acquaintance instead of an adversary.

It also allows you, if necessary, to remind them of what they said, a most impressive tactic if done in a sincere, friendly manner. "Well, Carole, in our last conversation you said that your banker gave you an approval for the loan and you were coming to my office. I never saw you. Can we reschedule that meeting? I have some cars here that are just what you were looking for."

A gentle verbal massage works a lot better than taking someone to task. "Hello Bob, we had an appointment. You never made it. My time is valuable. Let's reschedule. You better make it this time." Just the kind of appointment I'd be all excited to go to — right? Wrong! We are the professionals, not the customer. Always keep your cool.

If a potential customer is consistently disrespectful of our time then just give them up. But don't allow them to get to you to the point that you behave unprofessionally. Gently reminding a client of what he or she said can be a strong positive reinforcer. Chiding them and criticizing them gets you nowhere, sends them to your competition, and sends you to the attitude adjustment factory.

I'm not suggesting you be a marshmallow, but usually when a sales situation is not going our way, silence is golden compared with spouting out our negative feelings. Swallowing silence is a lot tastier than eating crow.

The ultimate feeling of success for me as a salesperson is when I've hung in and hung on, be it a week, a month or a year, and the customer makes a deal with me. None of it would have happened if I hadn't treated my business like a business with consistent serious follow up. A name and phone number scribbled on a message pad seldom survives a week, much less the extended period of time it takes some customers to buy.

The reason for the long-term monthly file is simple. They're gonna buy sometime, part of the time, anytime, sometime. Let's say it's January. Let's imagine you're in the car business. Customer A — Mr. Roberts — has just come into your dealership. You've gotten all the pertinent facts about his needs and wants. You have called him on three different occasions. He's always been receptive to your calls and on the third call the truth comes out. He can't buy a car until his income tax return comes back to him. He tells you he has an appointment with his accountant in the middle of February and he expects to get his return by the first of April.

Our first thought is to suggest he borrow against his return, but Mr. Roberts is an old-fashioned kind of guy who doesn't believe in that sort of thing. Your choices are simple. First, give him up as a prospect and chalk up your time as wasted. Second, suggest that he call you when his return arrives, which is basically the same as #1, but worse because you are asking him to do your job. Or, the third and most logical decision is to go to your long-term file and put his file card behind the month of April. Then go to your calendar date book and make a notation to call him March 15 to confirm that his taxes are on the way. Note that his card is filed for follow up April 1. Note the conversation and keep in touch. Tell him what your plans are, create an air of mutual obligation, then follow through.

Being credible is everything in sales. In sales, talk the talk, walk the walk and what goes around will come around. You may not close them all. You may at times feel unappreciated, cheated, disrespected and ignored. But if you're consistent, day in and day out, the sales bird of paydays will come to roost on your checkbook, in your savings account and, most of all, in the bank we call success.

If you strive for success and succeed, all the adjectives of success will follow. "The System" is self-propagating. When you first start out, you will have a skinny file box with a few cards in it that you will diligently tickle. Leaf through your box on a daily basis.

Sales are a numbers game. If you are diligent about your efforts, not giving lip service but actually applying yourself (only you know the latter for sure), your cache of clients will rapidly grow. Meeting and greeting is our job. Following up makes it a career.

In the course of a month many Mr. Robertses will want to buy in April, June or July. The point is they all buy sometime, whether it's a house, a car, a boat or cashmere coat. If we just nod our heads and let them go, we have wasted the time we just spent, wasted advertising dollars that may have created their interest, and wasted an opportunity we could be spending. Think about it. Personalize it.

Does it impress you when a salesperson politely follows up? Don't you feel a bit more obligated when they continue to persist politely? Wouldn't you rather buy from someone who is genuinely interested in capturing your business as opposed to the salesperson who waited for the 'up bus' to land? You jumped off the bus (got out of your car), made casual conversation, made either a whole- or half-hearted attempt to buy. He made a half-hearted attempt to sell. He might have taken your phone numbers and you never heard from him again or perhaps you got one half-hearted phone call. Did this create a warm feeling or rapport? Probably not.

It's true that some people won't care, some people will pour gas in the bowl of corn flakes you call your career and, without a second thought, set it on fire. You can't let them steal your heart and most of all you can't let them affect your attitude for any more than that moment. You might have two, three or four people not notice what a good, sincere job you've done. Ignore it. They are the water; you are the duck's back.

Take pride, take solace in the one out of four, one out of five, one out of ten who tells you, "After all the hard work, honesty and sincerity you've showed us, we couldn't possibly buy from someone else."

Now for the long-term domino theory of follow-up. Talk, file, follow up; talk, file, follow up; talk, file, follow up. Our entire business life is one long conversation directed at making deals with different people. We take the information and insights gained through these conversations and we file and follow up. Countless volumes have been written about unrewarded genius. Persistence and determination, however, will overcome almost any obstacle. Don't forget to ask for the sale, to request their business!

With consistent, persistent determination, we follow

up till the customer buys from us. Please note in that last sentence I didn't say "bought", I said "bought from us." If you are truly following up, then you don't give up. You may miss the first sale, sometimes circumstances beyond our control allow it. Sometimes another deal showed up first. You didn't have the inventory in stock at the time and other valid reasons beyond your control allowed the deal not to close. Does that mean you take the rapport, trust, familiarity and — most important — the time you have invested, roll them up in a nice neat ball and pitch it in the lake? I don't think so.

If it's a short-term deal such as a car, boat, some types of insurance, or suit of clothes, ask for referrals, find out how many cars are in the family, when they'll be buying again. Then follow up with a call ninety days or six months later. Send a note, drop a line. Stay in touch — it only takes time, which is what we have to give.

I know some in commission sales who work in a showroom sales floor operation would much rather talk sports, hunting, jewelry, spouses or politics with your colleagues, but when was the last time you got paid for doing so? I'm not suggesting you never come up for air and alienate your co-worker by being unfriendly or distant, but being a bit preoccupied with business is okay. It's what we're there for. Time is our natural ally; wasting time makes it an enemy.

As a salesperson, time is the commodity at our disposal, and we spend at least half our waking hours at work. Do you want to spend time with a friend or an enemy? Your job isn't a place to go to. It's an opportunity "to go." If sales are your game and time is your ally, then you should become a traveling mercenary of your time. When you're at work be loyal to your time and guard it well. When you're not at work, spend your time like money because you have invested it well while you were at your job.

With all that in mind, you're building your file, taking notes, keeping up, putting reminder notes in your daily journal, logging calls and information on your file cards and locking it together with the phone. Now, like a piece of property bought many years earlier, like an old farm in a growth corridor, your long-term prospects will start to show dividends.

If you have diligently filed names and turned them over into the long-term file when appropriate, you have started developing a cache of fresh names that reveals itself at the start of every month. Follow up every customer who was waiting for income tax returns, waiting for their house to sell, waiting for financing, or waiting for the last six months of their kids' education...and, an extra deal will present itself to us on a regular basis. These are self-generated with our time. Yes, sometimes we'll get fooled, disappointed and turned down, but we'll be in the game, not sitting in the stands second-guessing the quarterback.

Swing enough, throw enough, work enough, and

things get done. File them, call them, weed through them. Talk, filing and follow up always pay. Call them in sixty, ninety, one hundred and twenty, one hundred and eighty days. Stay in touch. Pull them out again in ninety days if you don't get an answer. Someone's going to buy. Are you going to sell?

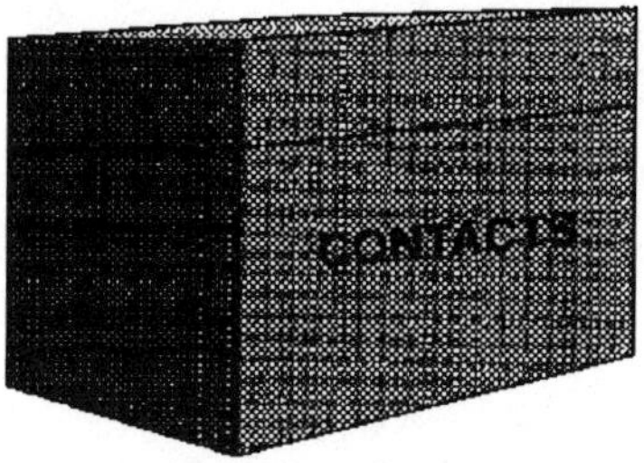

File Box

File Cards

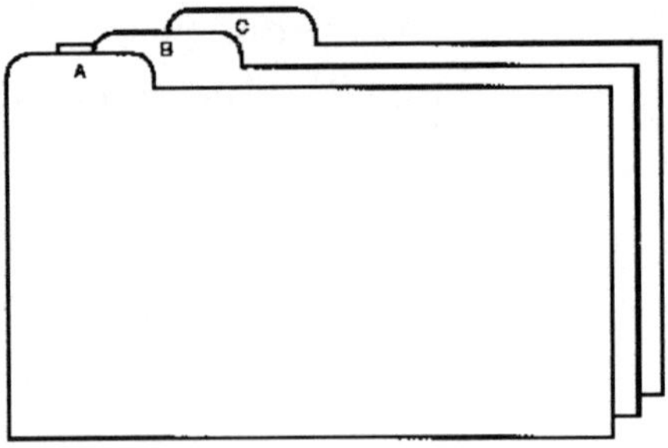

Alphabetical File Cards

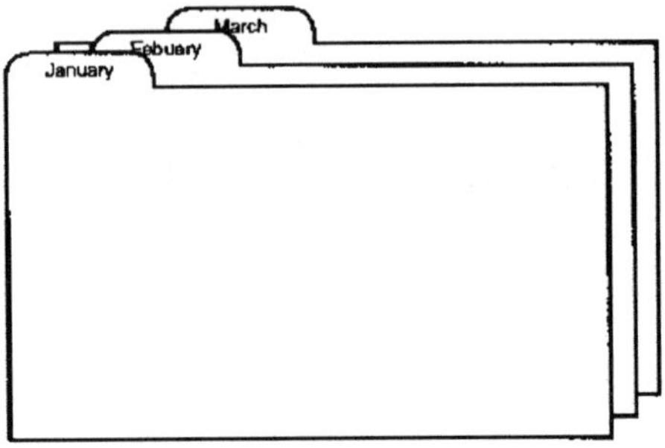

Monthly File

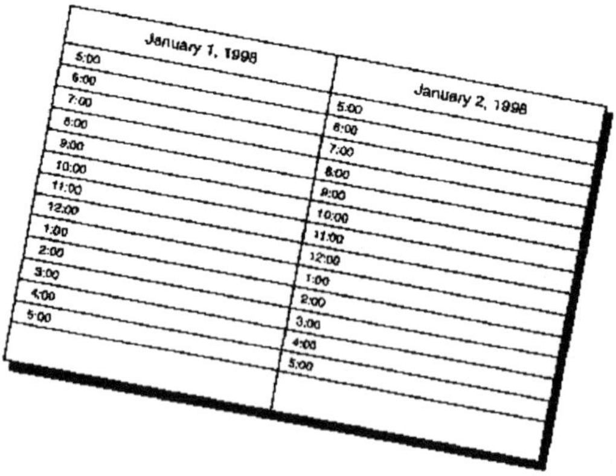

Appointment Book

If you are working with real estate investors or other investors who constantly buy and sell, the return on your investment of time could be many times over if you stay in touch. You can't win if you don't play.

If you do these things you will succeed, because 80 percent of your competition is doing nothing but waiting for fresh walk-ins and fresh phone calls. They are stacking the deck against themselves. They don't have their own business, they are just occupying space and time at someone else's business.

"The System" is mobile. If you go, it goes with you right under your arm. Remember the 80/20. Which section of that pie do you want? I'm sure you're not on a financial diet, looking to lose income. It's your right, your opportunity. Take your big slice — you've earned it. It's your deal.

Twelve

You Can't Win If You Don't Play

Not asking for the order
borders
on behaving like you're not there.

Ask for the order, go for the close, ask for a signature. Asking for someone's business is not rude or pushy. If you are in sales, it's the exclamation point to doing your job. Your conversation and professional demeanor should be like a funnel that leads to an opportunity to close.

Asking for someone's business is not out of line. In most unsuccessful sales opportunities, however, it is out of the ordinary. I am not suggesting you must hammer on someone until there is a flat spot on his forehead or put a gun to his back. Suggesting you would like to earn someone's business is neither of the above, unless you are behaving that way.

Treat people in a courteous, polite fashion and ask for the order. Put your best foot forward and ask for the business. Put a smile on your face, goodwill in your heart, determination in your spirit and ask for the sale. You can ask and still be a nice person.

Make a personal appeal and ask for the deal. Afraid of rejection? It goes with the turf, ask for the order. The customer is in a rush? Slow them down and ask for their business.

Don't be a chicken, ask for the sale. Throw a pass, or run — but try to get into the end zone.

A customer has objections? Find out what they are, set out to solve them, and then ask for the order. A customer has more objections? Nod yes that you understand; do everything you can to overcome them, and ask for the order. Any excuse will do to justify failure. Strive for the sale.

It is important that we truly make an attempt to empathize and relate to the quandary a sales situation can put some consumers in. This does not mean we stop doing our job. Sensitivity and empathy are positive traits in everyday life and powerful allies in any selling situation, as well as a positive way to ask for the sale.

What if are two powerful, effective words in any selling situation. I understand what you are saying, Mrs.

Consumer, the payment is too high. What if? You love the property but not the location. What if? What if...? And on and on.

People are starving all over the world and you have a chance to succeed. Ask for the order.

Are you looking for a perfect alibi as to why you didn't make a deal? Then don't ask for the order.

You won't make every transaction, but the odds get better when you take charge and try to close.

Asking for the sale is not a can of spray paint. It is more like broad, gentle strokes from a verbal paint brush that will allow us to change momentum while going back and forth, all the while attempting to coax a commitment.

If your technique needs work I'll share some with you in this book. Watch and listen to successful closers and get some ideas. Buy a book or listen to a tape on the subject; there are plenty to be found.

Try for the sale, strive to make the deal, ask for a signature.

These last two chapters have addressed what I consider to be bedrocks in the selling process. Consistent follow up, coupled with the ability to close the sale, is like throwing a large rock in at each end of a pool; the ripples of success will meet in the middle.

The past is a cashed check and the future is an unsecured loan. Ask for the order.

Thirteen

Anatomy Of A Close

Answer the door.
And close it behind you.

Some years back, one of my first sales managers, and a good sales teacher, said to me, "A good salesperson can't always tell you how they do it. They just do it." He was referring to sales instinct, to flying by the seat of one's pants, so to speak. There is truth in what he said, but sales skills are not simply a matter of genes.

Some salespeople, naturals, have a knack for saying the right thing at the right time. But I think, with patience, we can all learn to be "naturals" to a greater or lesser degree. Lack of confidence, fear of failure, fear of rejection — these are just some of the obstacles that can keep us from attaining the natural's greatest skill — closing a transaction.

Here are some closing thoughts for you. I think it is reasonable for a salesperson to assume that if someone did not want to buy and were not interested, they would not be at our place of business, or would not have invited us to their home.

- The "decision close." At its simplest, this means, "I've got the style, product, size or color you need. Do you want one or two?" A decision close is painless, smooth and no pressure. You've established that you have the product and they want it. "Which color, which size, which category do you prefer? Do you want to charge it or pay cash?" "We've established that you need life insurance, Mr. Adams. Would you prefer whole life or term?"
- The "payment close." You have qualified your customer and established the affordable payment parameters. You discuss down payment and terms, target the merchandise that falls in the established payment range and allow the payment to close the deal. This technique fits in nicely with the "decision close" if you can offer a choice in the payment range.
- The "commodity close." If something is hard to come by, rarely in stock, in short supply, a close-

out, end-of-the-line, a great location, or maybe you just like it, let your prospect know. Speak your piece. You never cared so much about your high school sweetheart until someone else took notice. Create urgency. Let people know what you have is a commodity.

- The "order pad" close. This is a dinosaur, but they still make hit movies about dinosaurs, don't they? In the "order pad" close the philosophy is: the more information you get on an order pad, the closer you are to a sale. You get a name and address for your own record-keeping on the order pad. The date, style and product are also gathered on the order pad. Do this in low-, no-pressure conversation. If the prospect will allow you to list equipment or accessories, you continue working down the face of your pad. The closer you get to the signature line, the better it is. You've got the price they want, the merchandise required and a document filled out that answers any questions in writing. "Just sign here."

This technique can be piggybacked with other closing styles, like the "decision close." The risk in this technique is that a savvy shopper may not close but want a copy anyway to shop your price against your competition. Pay attention. Don't be afraid to find objections. Search them out, if necessary.

You can't overcome a closing objection if you don't know what it is.

- The "follow-up close." Not every close happens right now, so for Pete's sake, if you tell someone you're going to follow up with them, do so. Lead by example. Do what you say and say what you do.
- The "silent close." This one is timeless. There comes a point where everything that needs to be said has been said. When silence is golden, don't lose that moment of opportunity by rattling on. You've said what is necessary and the table is set. Sometimes the best close is a passive one - the gate is open, let your client walk in. Too many cooks spoil the brew, and too much idle chatter can close the door on closing opportunities. Know what exit is yours and don't drive past it.
- The "qualified close." Another smooth, easy style. You qualify the prospect and in your mind you are sure you have what they want. Gently ask for assurance from them that if you've got it, they'd like to have it and then take them to it.
- The "customer service" close. This is powerful, but be sure you back up your promises. This close also helps to diffuse price, terms, payments and other objections. Service after the sale is powerful. Alluding to it and being able to show

awards or letters that indicate you do good work is a comfort to your customer and a powerful ally in any closing situation. Features and benefits always smooth the road to closing.

Identify with prospects. "Yes, I know it's a big decision, but you're going to do it sooner or later and it seems I have what you want. If it were me, I'd want to get on with it and then move on to the next project. All this time you're spending are valuable moments that belong to you. Do you really enjoy all this shopping around?"

Make a personal appeal for someone's business. This doesn't mean to plead or beg. It means to convey appreciation that the customer is in your establishment or dealing with you, and that you really want their business. "I'd really like to do business with you." "I really hope you buy this book."

Credibility is a powerful closing tool — what you will do for your customer, examples of those you have benefited in the past, how you can help, the amount of time you have been in the business, your own track record of customer satisfaction. If you're new to the field, cite your colleague's accomplishments and use the word "we." If you are working with an established company or brand name, base some of your credibility on theirs.

I have made many deals, large and small. However, the owner of my company made a huge landmark transaction, known statewide. When I am out on listing appointments I often cite this property as a deal "we" made at our firm.

The "surrender close" is made during negotiations. There is ebb and flow. Finally you say, with sincerity, "If I agree to this, then we've got a deal, right?"

Similarly, the "talk to your superior" close, when orchestrated properly, is strong. Just be sure that you have a reasonable assurance from the buyer that they will make the deal if the boss says okay.

These are just a few styles of closing. Stay upbeat and keep your closing language fresh. Don't fall into canned speech techniques. Take variations and change them in content, style and approach to fit the type of person you are dealing with.

I used the expression "closing thoughts." That's because closing is a thoughtful situation; it should be fine-tuned with mechanics and instinct.

In fast-track consumer sales, like appliances, shoes, cars, clothes and such, the odds are that many times you are only going to get one opportunity. They are not coming back, so short of being pushy and rude, try to make a deal, try to close. The best closes are not mere offers, they are decisions.

Fourteen

Get Over It

A cold wind beckons,
who would reckon
anyone would choose it
over a warm fireside hearth.

A deal goes sour, blows up, goes sideways. Feel the frustration, the irritation, sometimes even hurt — and let it go. Dwelling on a deal that failed means making your psyche carry a box of rocks. It robs you of energy and attitude, key ingredients to selling.

Look at it this way. We've all had a lot of trauma, hurt and pain. Some of it may have seemed insurmountable at the time. Now we're farther down the line of life, and we're still here. We've survived our personal doses of famine, pestilence and drought and made it through.

So what if you blow a deal? It's when we let that loss affect us negatively that we really start to multiply our losses. Some client or thoughtless customer has just made mincemeat of an opportunity and we in turn give the next five opportunities for success less than our best because we're in the woe-is-me gear.

You're going to get over it sooner or later. Sooner is better. That is, unless your idea of fun is sleeping on a bed of failed-sales nails. Don't allow the view from your windshield of success — that is, what's ahead of us, the opportunities yet to come — to be hindered by the rear-view mirror that holds our failures. The visions in that mirror are only as near as we let them be. Our attitude is like a selective concave mirror. If we choose to keep those negative objects close at hand they will stay closer than they truly are, and poison what truly is close at hand.

When was the last time you made a deal, made a new friendship or made wonderful love when your attitude about those things stunk? You're gonna get over whatever it is sooner or later anyway, so get over it sooner. Stewing in one's own juices is not a recipe for success.

The best hitters in major league baseball are successful only a third of the time. It is my experience that you must mentally keep yourself in the ball game of sales. Keep swinging and keep pitching. The hits and outs, strikes and balls are going to happen. So what if someone throws you a curve? Complaining about it solves nothing. Learning to recognize it and hit it keeps you in the game.

Deals have their unique characteristics and they all have similarities. Learn from your mistakes and learn from other people's behavior patterns. Observe, absorb and remember similar sales situations and learn from them. If a certain type of behavior on your part or a customer's sends up a red flag, don't ignore it. Respond to it. Utilize what has worked in the past. We may occasionally have to round off the edges, but we don't need to re-invent the wheel. Stay balanced.

Race, national origin and religion have no place in qualifying a buyer. I have known many salespeople who bore grudges against a whole ethnic group because of one or two bad experiences. Prejudice is unfair — and it will cost you money. How do you feel when someone says, with a negative tone in their voice, that all salespeople are the same, because they had a bad experience? It's not too fair, is it? Whatever it is, whoever it is, the sooner you get over it, the better off you are.

Fifteen

Big-Shot Disclaimer

Back when they were in missionary school
and found it easy to find all the tools
that would one day make them pope.

I've listened to scores of motivational tapes and read scores of books and articles by or about successful people. Some were uplifting, some were inspirational and some left me feeling somewhat hollow, or at the very least a little disconnected.

I think sometimes the writer has either achieved such a lofty status (or at least appears to have) that we "Joe Potato," everyday types find it difficult to relate. Let's face it, you try to improve your lot in life so you pick up a book or buy a set of tapes and the writer or speaker starts expounding on their personal wealth and success — the two or three million dollars they made last year,

Then there was the time I overpowered the hijacker and landed the burning 747!

the trips, the houses, the big deals, the stratospheric connections they have. All you were looking for was a leg up, and quite often these egomaniacal 'you-can-do-it-because-I-did-it' types are putting success out of touch and out of reality. A kind of "me-me-me" operetta.

You took the extra step, went out and bought the book, listened to the tape and maybe got inspired. Maybe you got some good ideas or maybe you just got a good dose of "me and my success and my money and my family and my life," and you wind up trying to figure out how you can reach a distant target with the small-caliber success gun that you're trying to lock and load. Meanwhile, the author is expounding on how he put the snow cap back on Mt. Everest when it was threatened by global warming.

Instead of feeling fired up you feel more frustrated than ever. Maybe it's a little envy, a little natural jealousy and human nature. Some of the inspirational success types want to sell books and tapes about how they did it, so you can do it, but they sprinkle in the gift of guilt. "How come you haven't done it?" is always a poor motivator. Sometimes it's true that we haven't put our best foot forward and applied ourselves, but not every time. Breaks, luck and timing often play a hand.

A large successful car dealer once said a fellow I know had a million dollars' worth of talent and twenty-five cents' worth of good work habits. If that's your problem, sections of this book, if applied, will help. They won't cure you, clear up your skin or put you on a diet, but they will help.

Often what the loftier-than-thou, self-elevated author or motivator fails to disclose is the "big break." I am not using this as an excuse for the rest of us to curl up in the fetal position and cite bad luck as a reason for mediocrity. However, I am taking to task some of these so-called experts from afar who don't tell the whole truth.

They neglect to mention that their small environmental company was failing and suddenly became an overnight success when the laws changed in their favor. Or that dad's farm was part of a site that Ford selected for a new plant prior to their family's real estate acquisition company being formed and capitalized. Perhaps their father-in-law owns the company or they just got lucky, picked up the phone and the right buyers or sellers presented themselves at the right time with the big deal.

Often the harder you work the luckier you get. That's fair, that's okay — just don't make yourself out to be a business king while neglecting to explain your birthplace.

I have a very successful acquaintance who probably would have been a success no matter what. But, when he told me his story of success, it started with one small house that he acquired, fixed up and sold for a large profit — leading in turn to more houses, more profits, more deals and more success — until he arrived at the millionaire status he holds today.

Gee, that's great. How come I hadn't done that yet? What he neglected to mention was the monetary lawsuit he won about the same time his career started to blossom. I never heard him give credit to his powerful ethnic connections and an established family name in business. Given his own considerable talents, he was able to parlay these things into a small fortune. His talent is always mentioned, but how about his breaks?

A former car salesman bills himself as the best, having sold thousands of cars — the most in the country. I'm sure he was very talented, but I also know that during his peak years he was a dealership within a dealership. By that I mean he had his own staff of assistants who would meet and greet customers and show cars and assist in paperwork and all the other time-consuming details. He was the closer. Does he mention this in his motivational speeches?

I read an article about a top national realtor. The article portrayed him as having single-handedly — with a little help from some assistants — selling 500 homes in one year. Ten homes a week! Superman in a three-piece suit, maybe, but what is more likely is what I heard from several other area brokers: Every sale made in his office, whether by him or an assistant, goes in his name; and that a large percentage of his sales are personal investment deals. When you're the big dog, and a talented big dog at that, you can afford to pay for some of your success. However, please don't hold yourself up as an example of success and wealth and only give part of the story. It's hard on the rest of us who are pounding, working and stretching ourselves to attain success and are wondering why we haven't hit it big.

I met a doctor while on vacation. I related this chapter to him and he shared his own big-shot disclaimer with me. When he was broke, struggling as an intern trying to make ends meet, one young intern was financially head and shoulders above all his peers — new car, new house, new clothes. He would constantly chide and lecture his associates about the merits of sound fiscal management and budgeting. My new friend told me that it was only later on at a social gathering that he found out the truth. The guy's father-in-law was filthy rich and bought his colleague and his baby girl the house, the car and everything in between. Surprise, surprise, surprise.

Many highly successful people out there are psycho success types. Success in business defines them, denotes them. It is their only line of demarcation in life, sometimes to the extent of giving up all else. Life is a globe filled with lines, latitude and longitude. Perhaps the reason for somebody's outstanding success and wealth is that they give up all the other lines of life and live on one track.

If it works for them, that's great. However, maybe your life includes success lines, social lines, fun lines, family lines, lots of life lines in general. When you work, work hard, define your line. Focus on it and you won't have to worry about what you haven't achieved yet, because it will come.

One extremely successful car dealer is known throughout the industry for the rages and tantrums he often directs at any employee who happens to be in the way. He's worth untold millions. I have never seen him smile. When he goes on vacation, he carries his company financial statement in the breast pocket of his beach coat and rarely speaks of anything else. Do I want his wealth? You bet. Do I want his temper, his attitude? No thanks. Do I want a work ethic that is so inflexible that when a long-term employee asked if she could temporarily adjust her hours to care for her mother who was dying of cancer, she was rebuffed in no uncertain terms and consequently quit? No, I don't think that is a trait I would want to emulate.

A few years back, I was having an inner conflict about being a success and a good human being at the same time. I was working at a large car dealership and had been promoted to a management position with considerable responsibility.

The name of the game was sell, sell, sell. Sometimes I felt I was making deals with people who couldn't afford what they were buying, even though they wanted it. My skill at making deals and getting the necessary financing arranged meant they got it. At times it wore on me. Yes, it was my job. I owed it to my employer to do my best, but as a human being, didn't I owe it to a fellow human being not to leave them financially strapped? I know it wasn't my job to baby-sit their finances, but when someone is in your office figuring their monthly finances to the last dollar, you should feel some empathy.

Given these mixed emotions, I went to visit my friend and confidant, the late, great Father Bob Skeris, an extraordinary priest at an inner-city church. He listened to my inner conflict of service and gave me some profound insights. He said simply to live life in balanced moderation. In parting he left me with five simple words to live by: "In the middle stands virtue." It is so right and so true, for there is a right and a left to so many decisions in life and virtue usually lies somewhere in between.

Sadly, Father Bob died six weeks later. One of the greatest privileges I've had was being asked to eulogize at his funeral. Father Bob wasn't a wealthy guy financially, but he was rich in spirit. He founded several halfway houses for alcohol and drug rehabilitation which saved lives and families. Success has more than one face, determination more than one suitor.

This book is intended to help make you more effective. I did not say to make your job easier. There is no easy way, but success makes our jobs — and the time we spend at them — a heck of a lot easier.

I want this book to be successful. That means helping you in your path to success, whatever that might be in your eyes.

In the language of life, it is critical to remember that money and possessions are only adjectives and adverbs. We are the nouns and verbs.

Sixteen

It's A Cinderella Story

Don't be fooled by barstool type stories,
no matter who tells them.

One way we can be the most unfair to ourselves is to listen to, and put stock in, get-rich-quick stories and schemes. If getting rich was easy, everybody would be doing it.

Overnight sensations are very rare, which is why they make such good fodder for stories. Don't be taken in. The dark side to these stories is that often those taken in by them tend to discredit their current state of employment by putting too much stock in these marvelous-sounding, rarely occurring, overnight success stories.

Every year some publication prints a picture of a 2,000-pound pumpkin with a child standing next to it. Don't be taken in by a 2,000-pound jack-o-lantern of a story. Beware of people making claims of success and attaching words in tandem like "fast," "easy," "short hours," or "anybody can do it." If someone discredits responsible positions in life to make their own seem better, beware. When things seem too good to be true, then they're usually not.

There is nothing wrong with dreaming and aspiring to financial success and greatness. Look around you. The vast majority of successful people did it the old-fashioned way — they earned it.

Cinderella stories are nice to hear. Heck, take a sixty-second vacation and put yourself in one if it makes you feel good. Just don't stay there.

Overnight sensations are like lottery tickets. Millions take a chance, very few cash in.

Seventeen

It's Your Money

Eenie, meenie, mynie, moe,
what should I
do with the dough?

When you make it, save it. Don't allow a big year, a big month, or a big week to alter your lifestyle in any substantial way. Commission sales are great. They are the best opportunity available for determining your own earning ceiling. But today's big deal does not guarantee a big check in the future.

There is nothing wrong with rewarding yourself for a job well done. Just be sure the rewards don't overextend you. A financial treadmill does not add to the quality of life. Being house poor, car poor, or boat poor because your income took a dip one year is no fun. Looking over

Har mateys, let's go spend those commissions.

your shoulder for the bill collector and fearing the delivery of the mail because of overdue obligations gets old real fast. When you make it, save it. Make sure that when your ship sails in, you don't leave it empty. Set some of the precious cargo aside.

I worked with a gentleman who at one time in his career was among the top Cadillac sales people in the nation. He was a top producer. During that period he built a large .home, raised a family and by all accounts lived the good life.

At the time that he and I were sales associates together he started to slow down. He was getting up in years and did not have the drive or energy that he possessed as a younger man. He still had a loyal clientele. He was dutiful and competent; the fire in his belly just didn't burn as brightly as it once did.

During this period the dealership that we worked at underwent some changes in management and operations. A new sales manager came aboard.

The new manager was young enough to be John's (not his real name) son. We all knew of John's past record, as well as his loyalty to the dealer. He had worked at the dealership for over twenty years. The new regime had been in place for a couple of months when I witnessed the following incident:

John's son was in from out of town and he and his father went out to lunch. John had taken an hour longer than usual. Because of that longer than ordinary lunch the sales manager was dressing John down in the middle of the showroom, in front of the entire staff. At the end of his tirade he informed a loyal twenty-year employee that if he did not like it, he could leave right now.

Why do I share this story with you? Because John's

options were limited and he was stuck. We had a heart to heart talk after the incident. He was devastated and humiliated. The problem was while he was making big money he was spending the big money. The years accumulated faster than his savings account. Now he was a senior citizen who had to go to work daily to keep up his lifestyle. He was in an unfortunate position.

The abuse he suffered at the hands of a moody, self-absorbed manager of my own age was a real eye opener for me. I told myself that day that I would never, God willing, be put in such a position at that age.

It's great to enjoy the fruits of our labor. Having options in our life is the tastiest of those fruits.

When you make it, save some of it. If you need some mentoring on this subject, I highly recommend *Financial Reality* by James McTevia. It's easy reading and offers sound opinions steeped in the real world.

Enjoy your life. Enjoy your money. And save some of both.

Eighteen

You Can't Dodge All The Cars Playing Both Sides Of The Street

A carnival barker reels us in
to play a game we just can't win.

If you always tell the truth, you don't have to remember what you said. In life, and in the business of sales, there is a line of demarcation, a defining point or points that separate truth from fiction. You can massage facts, maneuver details, harmlessly embellish product virtues. It was a brilliant shade of crimson, as opposed to red. "The property is a tremendous opportunity to create equity in your life," as opposed to, "The site has debt service cash flow." "That style of dress enhances your figure," instead of, "That loose fitting look hides your weight." "That sport coat broadens your shoulders," rather than, "The extra padding hides the fact you're a skinny bag of bones, Sir."

Which would you prefer — the forest green sedan or the aqua coupe? "They both are gorgeous," you say, even if neither of them appeal to you. It goes with the turf. There is a seat for every fanny; the customer's taste is not always ours, but the line of truth versus deal-making has not been compromised or broken. Don't cross the line, don't play in the traffic when it comes to lies.

Taking advantage of a lack of intellect and understanding that can threaten someone's well-being, or behaving in a manner you know is going to smell to high heaven, is no way to go. Selling a non-conforming piece of property to a novice, one that will set him back, wound him and leave him bitter cannot be justified with the excuse of "he should have checked." We all want to make the deal. However, when what we are doing fails the sniff test, which is, you can't hide the smell of a dead rat from yourself if you planted it there, change your ways.

The fact that you didn't know the engine had a rod knock — even though just before you sold it, you filled the crank case with super thick magic lube to quiet it down — has the sound of scurrying little rat feet all around it.

A lie is a fast-moving train that gains speed. No matter how much we remember, we won't remember it all. A lie can get to be like a long freight train filled with toxic waste. One lie leads to another and as the pollution spreads and the trestles weaken, that runaway freight train, with its cargo of misdeeds, lies and ill wind, is bound to derail.

When you start to fail at telling the truth it becomes easier and easier; turning back is hard, sometimes seemingly impossible.

Credibility is ours to lose, respect is ours to gain. The words "lying," "cheating" and "stealing" were not developed to define success and I know there are liars, cheats and thieves who are successful. They will never be held up as examples of how to live. They may have "stuff," but they don't have the "right stuff."

I remember having lunch with a dear friend, and as we were eating, an acquaintance of his came over to our table. I was introduced to him with a smile from my friend, small talk was made and he left. My friend turned to me and said, "You know how you can tell when he's lying?" "How?" I asked. He told me, "Every time his lips move."

Is that the kind of reputation you wish to build for yourself? I hope not. Truth is not a north-south highway. Truth does not change direction. The sun rises and sets in the same places. I don't think that the truth versus lies is any different. I don't wear a halo — neither do most of us. That doesn't mean we roll around in the muck of misdeeds, wearing them like fancy cologne.

Try to avoid the dirt of life. Wash it off regularly and if it gets to be a permanent stain, take a deep breath and ask yourself, "Do people just assume I'm lying?" or even more telling, "Do I just assume a lack of truth, a lack of integrity in my life and in my business affairs?" Understand the consequences. The traffic on a highway of lies may not get you today or tomorrow, maybe not for years, but odds are your reputation and honor will become a road kill that fades from a fresh carcass to a pile of unrecognizable fur in the roadside dust.

Nineteen

Among Ourselves

Rat-like ethics
will give a reputation
the odor of flatulation.

Honor among staff members is a major issue in the process of deal-making ethics. Call it stealing, skating, stiffing, cutting or any other name you choose. Deliberately stealing business from another person stinks. I've seen them all. From the brazen thief who steps in front of you and commits the crime, to the sneak thief who uses the time-honored excuse of, "But they didn't ask for you" (even though he or she watched you wait on them for an hour the day before).

Allowing a customer's indifference, lack of consideration or simple naivete to justify taking what is not ours is out of line. Customers don't determine our ethics, we do. I can't tell you how many times in my career someone went to lunch, went home or just took a well-earned day off and were taken advantage of deliberately by a colleague with convenient ethical amnesia.

I'm not sure which is worse — the rat who says, "He's out to lunch but I can help you," and proceeds to steal your deal, or the wimp who knows the customer was in earlier that day, but allows himself the freedom to make a deal because the customer was unconcerned about who his salesperson was. A quick, easy deal is made, but the person cashing the check is not the one who earned it.

Stealing a deal from an associate is no different than punching someone else's time card and collecting their eight hours' worth of pay. The fact is, I think it's even worse, given the high-wire nature of commission sales. Are you are professional salesperson, a professional thief, or do you fall somewhere in between?

The flip side of the unethical coin is the salesperson who spoke to a customer three weeks earlier, handed them a card, and walked away. No follow-up, no calls, no mail — but horns in on another salesperson when the customer wanders in weeks later. While not quite as insidious as the previous examples, they aren't much better. Typically what happens is that the customer becomes uncomfortable and leaves, and no one makes a sale. That costs both salespeople and their employer business that could have been gained.

There is no reason sales should not be an honorable profession. Unfair sales tactics poison a sales atmosphere. They negatively affect attitude, which is our most powerful sales ally.

As for management, most sales managers were once salespeople. A manager is supposed to be a leader. If you view unfair, unethical behavior among your staff with indifference or with the rationale of "as long as the deal gets made," you are an accomplice in a crime. There are shades of gray, but when it happens too often, gray becomes a bright pastel that is easy to recognize. Sales is only a dog-eat-dog business if we allow it to be, both as salespeople and sales managers. The standards that judge customer service have been raised. Why not keep the level of professionalism among ourselves high?

I could cite many more examples. Right is right and wrong is wrong. Whether it's suits, shoes, cars, insurance, houses — whatever you sell — if you have a choice, do the right thing. No deal is going to make or break you, but being labeled as a thief can. Do unto others as you would have them do unto you. If you don't like the taste of spinach, don't shove it down someone else's throat.

You can be remembered as a thief or as a class act. Your choice.

Twenty

Renewal

Wild fires burn and destroy,
much of the timber lives on.

No words were ever truer regarding business and sales than the words spoken by Scarlet O'Hara. "Tomorrow is another day." Think about how many worthwhile thoughts, plans, concepts and ideas have crossed your mind over the years.

Thoughts cross our minds and keep on going. They enter our minds from our own intellect and curiosity — worthwhile, sometimes even profound, ideas. If we don't grab hold, act upon them or write them down, they zoom right by us into never-never land.

We've all had great thoughts and ideas and allowed them to get away. Which leads me to this. If a lot of good stuff has gotten away from us, never to be thought of again, why does so much bad stuff that we have gone through become so ingrained in us, kind of like throwing back the big fish and keeping the small one?

In the business of sales, every prospect is a fresh start, an opportunity to turn over fresh soil with new results. Why do we keep going back to the same old, tired briar patch that we have reserved for our failures? Keep looking for, and discovering, those fresh garden spots.

Our attitude in life is a mirror to sales. Just like life, just like sales, "It's your deal." Assume you lost a deal right at closing time yesterday. In the morning on your way into work, you sling that "I lost a deal" knapsack on your back and then you walk into the office that morning. You might as well pick up your hand spade and go to work at the briar patch. Better yet, just go back to bed and pull the covers over your head.

Please understand, I have my own personally cultivated briar patch, like everyone else. It includes failed sales, broken relationships and plans have gone awry. It's not that I never visit it. But I never stay. Take a can of gas with you and when you leave, burn that sucker down. You don't fertilize crab grass, you put weed killer on it.

Life is an auction and you are the only bidder. How valuable are you to yourself?

You can't win if you don't play. If we only play on part of the field, the chances of scoring are much less. If that part of the field also contains the briar patches and booby traps of our failures, the chance for scoring becomes even worse.

It's a new day, a new deal. Grab life and run down field for renewal. It's like a football game — throw a long pass or a short pass. Run up the middle or go wide. Sure, you're going to be stopped at times; but, there will be scores, there will be victories. Nobody ever scores standing on the sideline.

Likewise, no one is going to raise the bid on life's auction except ourselves. Maybe the bidding has been stagnant for awhile; maybe it's even gone down. I say stick your hand up and raise your price. Hold one hand up with the other if that's what it takes.

The old deals are over. Stop turning over the soil in that prickly patch of failures and find a fresh spot to work on. Tomorrow is another day. It's your game. It's your auction. It's your deal.

Twenty-One

Broken Glass

Precipice ledges and cutting edges—
avoid them if you can.

Some people in this world, business people or otherwise, are accidents, mishaps and misdeeds waiting to happen, like a piece of glass left on the beach.

How do we spot these people and recognize them for what they are? Please note I did not say avoid them. Avoid is optional. There are times when you just can't get away from them. They are part of a deal you are trying to make, they married into the family, maybe you married into theirs, or they're your neighbor two doors down. Recognizing them, however, helps disarm them.

For the sake of this chapter, I'll focus on the business

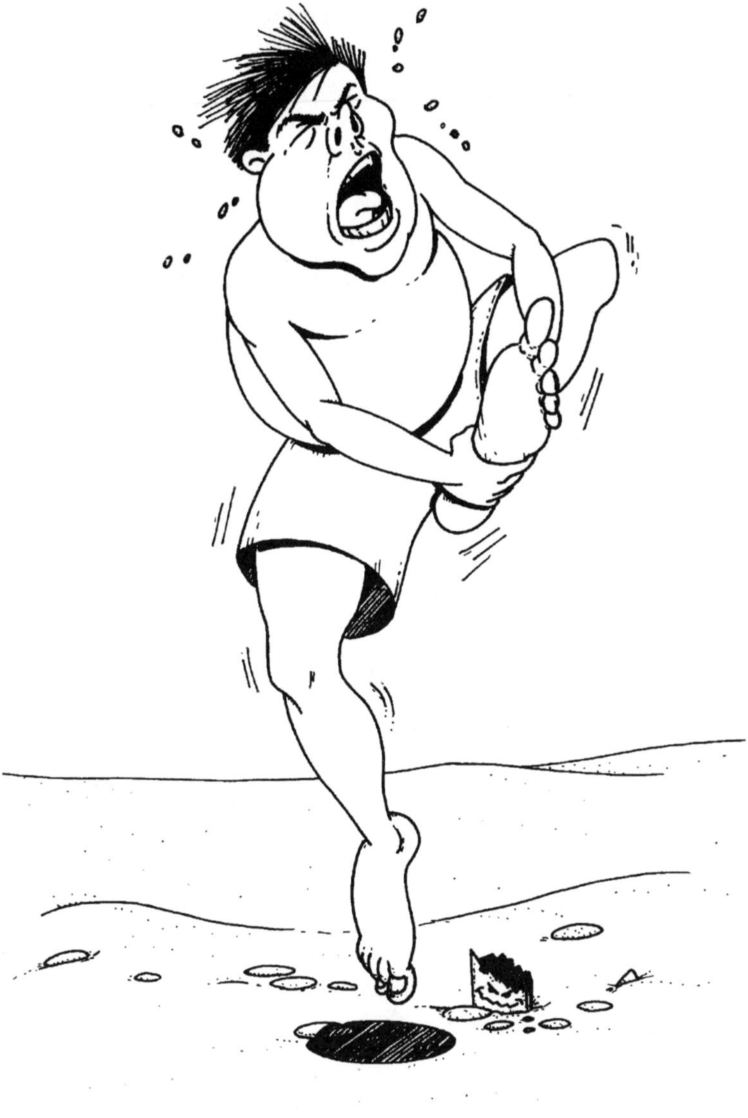

Gotcha!

side of the coin. No more accurate words were ever uttered than those of Shakespeare: "Me thinks he protesteth too loudly." Pay close attention to the person who constantly finds it necessary to espouse his own virtues of honesty.

My experience has shown, particularly in larger deals where there is considerable dialogue and many separate conversations, that a person who is constantly telling you, "Don't worry, you'll get your share, I'm sooooo sooooo honest," is getting ready to pick your pocket.

In smaller, short-term deals such as cars, there is usually just one large lie — after which you never see the party again. In a large deal breakdown or swindle, there is more dialogue and more time to plead one's virtue, thus convincing you to let your guard down.

I once did a deal with a fellow named Bob. I ended up referring to him as Saint Bob of Sunoco. He owned a service station I was selling on his behalf. He constantly told me what a great guy he was, that honesty was his trademark. He went so far as to tell me he was too old fashioned to be doing business in today's day and age, that he should have been born in an earlier, simpler time.

What I found out in the long run was that the only thing old-fashioned about Saint Bob was that he had the predatory instincts of a T-rex, that what he said and what he did were as far apart as Mexico and Montreal. The fact is, in Detroit many street signs were named after him. "One Way."

In Bob's world, it was always someone else's fault. I first met him after he had reneged on a transaction with a customer of mine. They had a handshake agreement based on honor — big mistake.

When the time came to close the deal, circumstances in Bob's life caused him to change his mind about the closing date. Of course, it was not his fault that his abrupt change of heart caused the buyer in this deal to lose thousands of dollars in deposits, legal fees and environmental studies. It was the buyer's fault for expecting to close on the agreed-upon date. In Bob's world, deals are made to be broken.

I came to the table with an offer after this fiasco. My buyer made a full price offer on a cash sale, just as Bob had demanded. Well, a funny thing happened on the way to sale. Bob created a huge smoke screen of distrust over some language in the purchase agreement, which could have been easily solved. By the time the smoke had cleared, the price had gone up a quarter of a million dollars. Surprise, surprise.

It wouldn't have been so bad if "One Way" was a consistent way. However, he was a constant turnstile of emotional and business upheaval. Terms for sale came and went with the day of the week. So much for Saint Bob of Sunoco and his old-fashioned ways. I wonder if in an earlier, old-fashioned, more naive world, his previous spirit ever met Shakespeare? What I am suggesting is "forewarned is forearmed." If "me thinks he protesteth too loudly" is constantly turning up the volume to define his virtue, stop and notice. If something seems too good to be true, then it's probably not true.

I know a dealer in the car business whose favorite expression is, "I just want to be fair." Translation, "I want it all. Hang onto your socks." I know another person who loves to say, "We just want everyone on the same page." Translation, "I'm not through writing that page yet. What you have just read is written in disappearing ink." Another favorite is, "We want you reading the same sheet of music." Translation, "It's my guitar, my drum, and what makes you think you can read music?" Or the time-honored expression, "You're preaching to the choir." Translation, "You can't understand me because I'm singing in Latin." My personal favorite is, "I want you to get everything you deserve, you've worked so hard." Translation, "Put your hands where I can see them, buster."

I would much rather deal with people who are straightforward and tough, who make me aware of their intentions to do the best for themselves right from the start, than the person who is looking to drop a pill in your drink and knock you out.

Sometimes broken glass comes out of nowhere. I was enlisted by a bank to sell a building for one of its clients. The building had been on the market six years without selling. I met with the owner and his faithful assistant. We discussed their situation. I analyzed the property and gave them my assessment. We agreed and listed the property.

In a magnanimous gesture due partially to their borderline deficit equity position and in deference to the referral by the bank, I volunteered to reduce my usual fee to help them out. BIG MISTAKE! I sold their building at almost full price in less than 90 days of market time. They had tried unsuccessfully for six years and I closed their building in less than three months. Part of our discussion was that upon the sale of their building, I would locate another site for them. Guess what? You got it. The result of my work was forgotten. Six years of fruitless marketing by them, out the window, check in hand, selective memory switch on, subjective reasoning full speed ahead. Translation, "Joe, you haven't responded to our needs like I expected." I'm still not sure which of the Great Lakes I said I could walk on. Please reference "disappearing ink transaction."

Unfortunately "What have you done for me lately?" can rear its ugly head virtually overnight, and in this case it took a bite out of me. Less than 48 hours after closing on the sale of a building in 90 days that had languished on the market for six years, I received a distasteful, disrespectful tongue-lashing and was informed that their business for the new location was "up for grabs." When broken glass is left on the beach, sometimes it can be underfoot and we don't even realize it until we're bleeding.

You are probably thinking that this deal was lost, and it very easily could have been. I had been wronged in such a way that I had no intention of going back for seconds, deal or not.

What I did was to turn them over to an associate. This kept the business in the company, and I got a share of the deal as a referral fee.

I'd like to suggest that when the magic goes away, when the rapport is history, or you have been stung too bad to go back, but you still feel a viable deal is there to be made, turn the customer over to an associate. Part of something is better than all of nothing.

Inform your colleague as to what has transpired and give them an opportunity at the situation. It is better business for yourself and for the company, as well as your associate. It doesn't matter whether it is boats, cars, planes, real estate, or whatever you're selling, if your instincts tell you there is a deal to be had, and you're just not the one to make it, let someone else step in. It is like putting a relief pitcher in a baseball game. It is the professional-thinking way to handle things.

Optimism, a good attitude and hard work are always a good recipe for success. Unfortunately, sometimes it takes a dash of realistic cynicism to make the bread rise.

Twenty-Two

Cats, Dogs, The Zoo And I

Zoo do, who do,
a chance, a shot,
you do, we do,
likely as not.

Out of every adversity comes the seed of an equal or greater benefit. This chapter is about a proud accomplishment in my life that came about as a result of true sorrow and loss.

I'm an animal lover — dogs, cats, horses, wildlife. I take great joy in them all. As a child and as an adult I have brought home strays, found homes for the homeless and have felt deep sorrow for the oppressed — humans, pets, it doesn't matter. I love National

Geographic specials. I hate to see a baby lion starve, but take no satisfaction when the lion's mother kills a gazelle so it might live. Life is full of paradoxes.

This is a very personal chapter and I am going to invoke the big-shot disclaimer clause right now. I never made a dime being an anonymous godfather to hundreds of homeless cats and dogs who otherwise would be dead and buried, but it ranks as one of the peak moments in my merchandising life. Through it, I and the events I helped found became the subject of numerous stories and publicity, locally and nationally. It all started rather innocently. I read an article in the *Detroit News* about a major animal shelter which was forced to euthanize 90 to 95 percent of the animals it took in because of a lack of animal adoption candidates.

The vivid description of kittens, puppies, abused cats and dogs that faced death every day with no chance for adoption brought tears to my eyes. The article also discussed the trauma that the constant euthanasia wrought on the workers at the shelter. I felt compelled to try to make a difference.

I called the shelter, which shall remain nameless. They know who I am and most in the animal rights community know who they are. In the article, their location was prominently mentioned as a reason for poor adoption performance. I offered them my services as a real estate broker pro bono. I offered to donate my entire commission toward the down payment on a new location and suggested I could help raise funds for the balance. Initially my offer was received enthusiastically. However, the shelter failed to follow up.

I continued to call them offering help because the story of the helpless animals haunted me. I had several conversations with the director of the shelter, but they led nowhere. This seemed rather contradictory to me. You have a big problem, I want to help you solve it, yet the subject keeps being dropped.

I think eventually the group tired of my persistent effort to improve their conditions. You can lead a horse to water but you can't make it drink. You can give someone the tools but if they don't want to use them, the house won't get built.

Finally the director's husband, an attorney (kind of figures, doesn't it?), called me and said that while they appreciated my offer of locating a better adoption site, I was naive about their mission and they would be unable to utilize my talents and fundraising abilities for such a venture. What he did suggest was that I could volunteer at the shelter cleaning cages and doing some clerical work. He thanked me for my time and hung up.

Somehow all that seemed a bit misplaced. If an impact player like Barry Sanders offers to take the ball and run with it, I don't think you make him a blocking back or, worse yet, sit him on the bench. Back to the horse and water analogy.

I stopped pursuing the subject with them, although

the story in the paper and the constant death march through their shelter still haunted me.

At the time, I owned two cats, Jam and Hayes. Jam was on his way to an animal shelter when a chance call from a friend's wife united us. Hayes, a stray named after the street on which I found him when he was six weeks old, malnourished with no hair left on his tail in the dead of winter, was my other cat.

Hayes is a calico who is full of hiss and vinegar. Jam was my gentle giant, 30-inches long from the tip of his nose to the end of his tail. He was loving and loud, following me everywhere with a full-time conversation of meows and purrs. He had large paws, like small ping-pong paddles, long, shiny black fur, yellow eyes and a star on his chest. He had kitty movie star good looks. (Of course, we all feel that way about our pets and children.)

Jam was a rambler and a rover. I lived on a quiet street and he spent a lot of time outside. One night, he never returned. After several days of searching local animal shelters, leaving reward signs and searching streets, we found him, killed by a car. I was devastated. After 11 years, he had become family. My heart was broken.

After awhile I decided to get another kitten. I immediately decided to go to the shelter about which I had read. Maybe they didn't want my help, but at least I could save an animal that otherwise would be doomed to death because of their poor location and adoption statistics. I drove 30 miles to get there, although other shelters were much closer to my home.

What came next was a scene so absurd you would have thought Arlo Guthrie wrote it as a sequel to "Alice's Restaurant." I entered the shelter with a warm heart and a pocket full of money in case medical expenses were needed. I was greeted indifferently upon explaining that I was there to adopt a kitten. I innocently explained the tragedy that had befallen Jam, my gentle giant. I told the shelter manager about my previous offer of help and that it was still available. I wandered among the cages. After some searching and heart-wrenching guilt about the kittens I couldn't take home, I settled on one.

The adoption application was filled out and I was asked to wait in the lobby. After phone calls to my vet to confirm I had treated my cats with shots in a timely manner (I had) and a review of my personal character and background, a verdict was rendered. I was told I was an unfit pet owner because my cat had been killed by a car. My adoption efforts were rejected.

At first I was dumfounded. Then I was angry. Almost all of the cats they took in were destroyed. My cat had 11 years of love, affection and premium food, but I was unfit. I looked at the kitten in the cage who could not come home with me and wondered why destroying it was a better option. I tried to explain how the kitten would be fine and about the help I had offered to the shelter. "Hey, I'm okay!" I might as well have been talking to a plant.

The crowning blow came when I asked for my personal application back and they refused to return it. I later learned it would become part of a permanent file of unfit pet owners.

I was angry and devastated. I immediately drove to a public shelter near my home where I was received with open arms. I conveyed my story of rejection which was received with amused amazement, signed papers agreeing to treat my new kitten kindly and to spay her, and took the new kitten, Lily, home.

I was still seething. I called the society director (whose home phone number I still had from my previous efforts of help) and asked her about my adoption rejection and treatment. She reiterated that due to my cat's death I was deemed unfit. When I protested and reminded her of her shelter's poor record of adoption rates, she attacked me with a chilling statement so cold in its disregard of my feelings it hurts to this day.

She said it was better to euthanize the animals in her shelter than to risk their death by being hit by a car. I persisted, reminding her of my cat's long, happy life, suggesting that her example was rather extreme compared to 72 hours in a shelter and sure death by injection.

Her response was to ask me how many cars ran over my beloved Jam before he finally died. I felt like I had stepped into a backyard with a vicious pit bull I didn't know was there. This cat was my friend, my surrogate, four-legged child. Talk about cruelty. I realized I was dealing with an emotional terrorist who just didn't give a damn.

Time went by. My new kitten grew healthy and strong, but I was still haunted by the thought of constant death in the shelters. What could I do to help?

Not long afterward, a new, enlightened zoo director came to our town. I read an article about how he abhorred euthanasia for healthy animals and the seed of an idea was born. What better place to adopt animals than from a zoo? Families go there, people who are caring and interested in life.

Let me come up for air here. I know some of you are saying, "So what? What does this have to do with making deals?" Let me suggest this. The ability to make a deal is no different than the talents of a carpenter, plumber or engineer.

How many times have you heard heartwarming stories about people pitching in for improvement in a community, for a church, a school, an underprivileged family? If a carpenter can donate time to rough in a school building, why can't an entrepreneur lend time and gray matter in his area of expertise to provide his community good, promotional fund-raising and sales concepts? They are just a different type of mortar and stone.

When it comes to community involvement, we all

have our special niche or talent. Never sell yourself or your community short. Coaching, counseling, driving the elderly, saving cats and dogs — it all puts breath into the community.

Back to the zoo. On a cold, snowy night at the dealership (at the time I was a sales manager at a large metropolitan car store) I received a return call from the director of the Detroit Zoo, Ron Kagan. I had cold-called him earlier that day and left my phone number only half-believing he'd call back.

I gave him a thumbnail sketch of the animal shelter story and my idea. Much to my delight, we set up a meeting to discuss matters further. The man I met was as much like me as he was different. What sets him apart from so many people in lofty, insulated institutional positions was his entrepreneurial spirit, his risk-taking abilities, and, most of all, his good heart.

We had a great meeting. My original plan was a full-time brick and mortar shelter. He suggested that was a future possibility, but how about we start with a day on a weekend? Part of something is a lot better than all of nothing.

I conducted interviews with a number of shelters and, in the end, a chance rescue by myself and the Michigan Humane Society of a stray dog trapped on the freeway led us to join forces — the zoo, the Humane Society and a deal maker. A lot of fences were mended and politics put aside to create "Meet Your Best Friend at the Zoo."

New best friends.

Both sides bent a lot to make it happen just like any large deal, and when there wasn't enough bending, the middle man deal-maker was there to massage or muscle parties to the table, as with any deal.

The stage was set. The first event was a one-day affair, complete with television, newspapers and guest celebrities. The organizers were nervous, but excited. The end result was success beyond our wildest dreams, a record achievement. One hundred animals found homes in one day. It was by all accounts a smashing success.

Success is like a water table rising to its own level. Just

because you sell 25 units in one month or 30 properties in one year doesn't spell the end. Success should always be the start of something good. It's not the end of one deal, rather, the opportunity to build towards the next deal, the next opportunity.

We immediately made plans for the next event. To further enhance our opportunity for success, we employed the retail concept of networking among the various animal welfare groups. Up to that time, most of these groups had been working their own turf with little communication. Like anything in life, if you can get like-minded people to put aside their differences and discover instead what they have in common, you can create a powerful force. I like the Bible expression, "Wherever two or more are gathered in my name..."

The second event was a barn burner. We found homes for more than 400 homeless animals.

The third "Meet Your Best Friend at the Zoo" set the standard for the nation. In two days, 572 homeless animals whose lives were at risk went home. We had become the largest adoption event in the United States and probably the world. "Meet Your Best Friend" has become an annual tradition at the Detroit Zoo, saving the lives of thousands of homeless animals. Old dogs, fat cats, a three-legged dog, a one-eyed kitten and many others have found a new lease on life.

Yeah, this was my deal, but it just as easily could have

been your deal. What good ideas, thoughts or aspirations have you buried or set aside lately?

I want to reiterate that none of this would have happened without going into action. My action, the zoo's action, the Michigan Humane Society, our sponsors and all the groups and people who pulled together to make it happen. Thanks to all of them, I got to be an anonymous godfather to a bunch of cats and dogs.

What about that original group that spurred me to action? I tried to bury the hatchet and we invited them to our third event. They turned our invitation down. Some people take longer to come around than others. I hope someday they change their minds.

"You think dogs will not be in heaven?
I tell you they will be there long before any of us."
ROBERT LOUIS STEVENSON

Twenty-Three

Books, Covers And Assorted Stuff

Reciprocity, synchronicity:
given a chance
things unfold as they should.

"Never judge a book by its cover." We all know that. It applies to sales, deals, and life in general.

You may have a meeting with a client dressed to the nines — big car, fancy jewelry and a debt-to-income ratio that is 100 percent and rising. On the other hand, you may greet a man with dirty hands, driving a dirty truck, speaking in monosyllabic tones and assume his income is as small as his vocabulary. Actually he is taking a break to shop at your store. He owns a welding firm.

He learned his trade in vocational school, employs ten dirty guys like himself and doesn't owe anyone a dime. He may not read or write well, but he sure can count. Now, who would you rather be spending your time with?

I learned my lesson early on. As a young man in high school, I sold shoes at a fashionable women's clothing store. There was a fair amount of traffic and some of my fellow salespeople would try to pick the buyers by their appearance.

I had been on the job for a couple of weeks and was still the rookie on the floor. Everyone was busy except two of us. Two ladies walked into the department at about the same time. One was a frail, matronly black lady rather meek in demeanor, dressed in a plain cotton dress. The other was a flashy, well-dressed white lady.

I remember the scene clearly; it was one of those defining moments in my life when a light went on and, ah-ha, crosses your lips in retrospect. The flashy lady was confident to the point of haughty. She beckoned for one of us to come over pronto, and my associate raced over, leaving me standing at the gate.

As he left, he snickered a bit at leaving me with my "plain Jane" customer. My client had quietly sat down and was waiting her turn for service. I was too green to know any better and after greeting my customer, I followed her directions and proceeded to the back stock room to retrieve a pair of sturdy walking shoes in her size.

Meanwhile, back in the stock room, my colleagues

were chortling together over how Pete had gotten the "good" customer and stuck me with an old lady who wasn't gonna buy a thing. Lo and behold, she said she would take those "Air Step" walking shoes and then she turned her attention to the Ferragamos display. They were the most expensive line in the store.

As I stood by attentively, she searched the display, checking prices and clicking her tongue at the expense. Finally she turned to me and asked to see a pump in her size. She tried it on, told me to leave it with her, then went back to the display rack. We went through this scenario several more times. Each time she would click her tongue at the price, ask me to find it in her size and then send me back for another. She had still not committed to anything but the first pair of walking shoes. Meanwhile I was building a fortress of boxes housing expensive shoes around her.

Finally she looked around her at the assembled boxes. With the sweetest twinkle in her eyes she explained to me how she really didn't like to shop for shoes, but when she did, she liked to buy good shoes that would last. Then she thanked me for being such a patient young man, pulled a store charge card out of her purse and said she would take every pair.

Her charge card was from our store but it was different from any I'd seen, covered with flowers and floral colors. My manager explained to me that it was a VIP card reserved for only the best customers.

Meanwhile, my associates stared at all this in disbelief. The flashy buyer had bought one cheap pair of sandals and left. To make matters worse, she returned them for a refund later that day.

My manager and I walked my customer out to her car, where we helped her load eight or ten pairs of the best shoes we carried into her back seat and left. After she drove away, he looked at me and said, "Wow, you sure are going to make a good salesman."

Actually, I was simply smart enough not to outsmart myself and knew enough not to have learned how to qualify a customer from 30 feet away — a lesson I carry with me and practice to this day. I never did get to wait on that sweet little lady again. In fact, I never saw her again. But the lesson I learned, the ah-ha that sunk in that day, will stay with me and, I hope, you, for the rest of our working days.

Twenty-Four

Sophie's Choice

A time to go,
we never know,
spirit referees life.

You have to practice what you preach. In this chapter I'd like to share with you the favorite follow-up story of my career. It happened because of consistent persistence. It also came about in no small part because my customer respected my efforts and recognized that a salesperson was taking his job seriously.

At the time I was selling Cadillacs at a large metropolitan Detroit dealership. I received a sales call and from the questions asked during the telephone conversation, I got the impression that I was speaking with a serious, qualified buyer. I took the gentleman's name, address and phone number, made notes on the conversation and started the follow-up dance. I dropped a brief note in the mail, transferred my notes to a follow-up card and went to work.

Please note that not every prospect is going to walk in the door. Some of our best opportunities come via the phone on sales call-ins or ad response. These can and should be followed up with the same diligence as a personal meeting. If they called because of an ad, not only are they shopping, but the ad cost our company a pretty penny. We might as well get a bang out of our buck, so to speak, and if we or our firm is spending the money to create advertising response, it is a waste of time and money not to follow up on a strong sales call.

Giving someone prices and information and saying please ask for "Larry" if you stop by is not much of a plan. Not only that, but if you take it a step further and think about the money spent to generate that sales call, you might discover that each of those calls cost you or your firm $20, $50, $100 — or even more — when divided by the amount of money spent to generate it.

Advertising is not inexpensive. Some of our best opportunities come via the phone; treat them seriously. Sales calls are a numbers game. Time is our ally. Treat sales calls seriously and a fair share of them will come to roost in our wallets in the form of closed deals.

Okay, I'll climb down from my follow-up soapbox and return to the story. I followed up with my prospect a few days later. He hadn't bought anything yet and I continued to stay in touch. Our conversations were brief and friendly. This went on for several months. Time is our ally. Spend it on business and business will come.

I knew this man was qualified. He was an executive with a large firm and lived in an upscale neighborhood. This information was garnished through simple questions and asking for an address to send correspondence. It turned out he was qualified to buy a Cadillac. He also was qualified to buy a Lincoln at another dealership, and he did just that. I found this out in one of my subsequent follow-up calls.

It was very disappointing. We had many friendly phone chats and although we had never met we had established a good rapport. What to do? Throw his card away in disgust? Get mad? He apologized to me and said he got a great deal through a friend who was a Ford executive and that it wasn't going to be his last auto purchase. He was still going to buy a Cadillac Eldorado sometime in the future. I asked for referrals and said I'd call him in a year. I put him in my long-term monthly tickler file. By this time we had been talking for six or eight months, and although we had yet to meet in person, we both felt like we knew each other.

A year passed. His name came up for follow up in my long-term file and I contacted him. He was still driving his Lincoln but he said to call him in a few months and that he would probably be ready. His card went back in the long-term file and when three months had passed his name came up again. When I called his office and asked for him, the secretary hesitated briefly and then gave me the news that he had died suddenly a month earlier. I hung up the phone feeling I'd lost a friend I'd never met.

Six months passed and I was at my desk working when a page from the operator informed me of a customer in the showroom to see me. Upon our introduction you can only imagine my surprise. The lady who introduced herself to me was the man's widow. Her name was Sophie. She told me her late husband had said if he ever bought a Cadillac Eldorado, his dream car, he was going to buy it from Joe Sowerby, some guy he'd never met but who he'd been talking to for more than two years.

Of course, she was still grieving the loss of her husband, but it was time for a new car. She was going to buy the Cadillac her late husband always wanted. She considered me his salesman and subsequently her salesman. She told me she couldn't imagine buying a Cadillac from anyone but me. Needless to say, I made the deal.

I sold her another car a couple years later. When I left the car business and went into real estate, I listed and sold some property for her as well. There is nothing more effective than disciplined follow-up to make time your ally. I don't expect, nor do I hope, to get any more referrals from the grave.

Working steadily and following up has its rewards.

Consistent persistence pays off! I'm sure my late customer's spirit was smiling at the turn of events all of our phone conversations led to.

Remember the philosophy of follow-up — they buy or they die, and every once in a while they still may buy.

Twenty-Five

The Package

Maintaining the machine
is a worthy scheme.

I want to suggest that — if possible, and you give it a chance to succeed — physical exercise at any level is a terrific investment. Five minutes or five miles, either is better than none. It can pay off both mentally and physically. Taking the time to take care of your body can be like conducting your own motivational seminar. It can feel like making those last couple of sales calls at the end of the day (when all you want to do is go home) and — surprise — making a deal.

You don't have to go to extremes unless, of course, you want to and your health will allow you. At this time I wish to invoke the BIG-SHOT DISCLAIMER clause and use myself as a reference point because I'm the only fitness and navigational compass to which I have intimate access.

In my extreme edges on both sides of the fitness envelope, I went from running marathons — racing every weekend and being a religious daily runner — to staying out late, partying and taking an occasional jog. Very occasional. What I have found is that my edge is a bit sharper when I am exercising on a regular basis. No, I didn't fall apart and my business didn't go to pot when I didn't exercise much.

I will say this. The subtle feeling of confidence and self-respect that a lonely morning run gives me creates an edge that lasts all day. Your poison may be a treadmill, aerobics, stair master, roller blading or any other workout that gives you that tingle of quiet confidence. The point is — tickle it.

When I sit down behind my desk, showered, shaved and a few miles under my belt, how can I not have a rolling start advantage over a regimen that consists of toilet, sports section and three cups of coffee? It's unleaded regular against jet fuel!

You say your schedule won't allow a morning workout. Afternoon and evening sessions are great for unwinding and a positive note on which to finish the day.

Yes, I know accidents happen. I could get hit by a car or I might get bitten on the butt by a big dog. Those are accidents inflicted upon us by outside sources. A far worse accident is the one we see in the mirror waiting to happen. Bad diet, bad habits and 30 pounds overweight is an accident waiting to happen, and our hand is on the steering wheel.

Do what you can, do what you must. Say your knees are bad, and so is your diet. You can solve at least one of those problems. No, it's not easy — neither is being a success — but it can be very gratifying. Let me state clearly that I'm not trying to be preachy or holier than thou. A tip is a tip.

You gotta do what you gotta do. The same goes for me. However, there is no arguing the point that excess weight is harder on your system, harder on the body that surrounds your system and, more times than not, hard on your head and your self-esteem. Physical conditioning is easier on all of the above. We are the package, our only package. Conditioning the body nourishes the head and releases the body.

Creating a sharp edge to our minds and letting all the angles of our body go soft and round isn't much better than becoming a gym rat who never learns to read or write. It's a package deal.

Getting in shape, much like a better income or a long-term investment, often requires delayed gratification. They all take time. Overnight sensations are rare, but as in most of life, defined persistent effort pays off. I'll go a step further than that and say there are not many guaranteed investments. Investing in your health and physical welfare is a guaranteed winner every time!

Twenty-Six

Batteries Not Included

The same game,
different names.

This is a touchy, tricky chapter to write. God, Buddha, the ultimate spirit — whatever name you choose — can be an asset in your life. If God is in your life, then God will be in your business. Enough said.

Twenty-Seven

To Lunch Or Not To Lunch – That Is The Question

If lunch
Leads to crunch.

In many places of employment, the line in the sand over hard work is drawn on whether someone takes a lunch hour or not. Some people never go to lunch and wear the fact like a "red badge of courage" for hard work. For some this is accurate, for others it doesn't matter. Some people work hard and have an ethic in that direction, lunch or not. Others are out to lunch regardless of whether they are eating.

As I have continually stressed throughout these

pages, it's not time spent at the job, it's time doing on the job that counts. This chapter may seem a little tongue-in-cheek, and in some ways it is. In some ways, it's not.

Over the last 20 years, my lunch habits have varied. At times the newspaper and a bite to eat were fuel in my tank. At other times a sandwich at my desk and a pen in my hand served the same purpose. There is no formula for such aspects of our life. I would suggest that it is what works best for you at the time.

If you need the break, want the break, deserve the break, would resent not taking the break, by all means do so. Enjoy and take advantage of it. If you are going to worry about the break, worry about being gone — if it creates anxiety, guilt, worry or concern — then stick around.

I was going through a very painful period in my life where my job was my anchor while another part of my life was getting flushed down the toilet. I didn't take many lunch breaks. It was what worked for me at the time. A good part of my business career I have taken a lunch. I worked hard, worked steady and a break from my desk fired me up for the balance of the day. If lunch is important, use it as a reward system for yourself. Never use it as a form of punishment. Take it if you need it

All this counsel goes out the window if it's politically incorrect to take a break. If the boss never lunches out and the staff never lunches out and you like your job,

But it was only a teeny weeny lunch hour.

then you never lunch out. Don't provide the paint and brushes to put a bull's-eye on your heiney. If you like your job, the money is right and going out to lunch is an issue, then don't leave. If it becomes too much of an issue to you, then move on. Don't make yourself a target by deliberately going against the grain. Most places of employment don't operate this way. But if what you are reading rings a bell, pack a lunch or keep some carry-out menus in your desk.

Keeping your nose to the grindstone will only give you a flat spot on your face. Taking a regular breaks for lunch, or not, seldom determines one's ultimate success. Being steady, consistent and enthusiastic at a personal level about what you do is more likely to be the straw that stirs your success.

Twenty-Eight

Walking Papers

Hired, fired — conspiracies at will.

Big shots and little shots, corporate heads, hourly employees, world leaders, major sport figures, Sparky Anderson, Lee Iacocca, Billy Martin (countless times), Yogi Berra, Casey Stengel, President Bush, President Carter, Bill Russell, the entire Eastern Bloc Communist regime and more. The best of the best and the worst of the worst can be pink-slipped. Big people, little people, people in between, and me — Joe Sowerby.

This is a hard passage for me to write. Hopefully it will be a rite of passage. Every situation is unique to itself.

When I interviewed prospective employees, I told

them the hardest parts of my job were hiring and firing, but that I did them both. I was uncomfortable hiring because often prospective employees bared their souls to me. They gave me insight into personal affairs, reasons they needed the job — perhaps they were in a bad way financially, or some private personal crisis put them across the desk from me in this interview — all in an effort to get hired. I often felt people were baring details of their life to me in an opening conversation that I had no business knowing about. It made me feel uncomfortable, uneasy and in some cases, sorry for them. I was always attentive; however, it didn't necessarily get them hired.

I don't enjoy rejection, so I am rather sensitive to it, whether I am receiving it or giving it. Firing someone, I often thought, was as hard on me as them. I lost sleep over the decision to let someone go, perhaps turning their life upside down. I know there are some bastards out there who relish that power surge. It never gave me any satisfaction.

So let's get to the point — I got canned! How do you fire someone who showed the strongest profit margins in your organization? How do you terminate someone who has carried your operation for the better part of five years? I guess it's not that hard. The dealership I worked for once spent $25,000 to hire a large consulting firm from California to review the store's needs and improve performance. When it was time for my evaluation, the representative of the firm introduced himself to me and then said, "So you're the star of the company." That's what their analysis had shown them, but I got fired anyway.

When I was hired, the department I took over was a big loser. During my tenure, my employer built a large new department facility in response to spiraling profits. We did millions of dollars in sales and many hundreds of thousands of dollars of profit. So why did I get my walking papers? Well, it takes two to tango.

There had been a behind-the-scenes power struggle going on between myself and another sales manager with more seniority employed by the dealer. We were oil and water. As I said many times during my employment there, the owner liked me but he loved Tom (not his real name).

My associate manager was famous for throwing uncontrolled tantrums. I never did. My department's bottom line was always more profitable. It didn't matter. I had a picture of my brother on the wall of my office. He is a highly respected economist and his picture had appeared on the front page of a local paper. For no reason at all, my associate walked in one day and took it down. He said he was tired of looking at it. The picture went back up, and so did the tension. Power is a funny thing, but that was his style. His behavior didn't seem to faze the owner. He had made his choice.

As time went on, my dissatisfaction and distaste of the

situation became more apparent. I can be opinionated, headstrong and obstinate. I had carried the dealership for years. I know my business, worked hard and did not respond well to tampering. All those traits are tolerable if you own the store. If not, watch out for those trapdoors.

My demise was just a matter of time. I was actively considering a number of alternatives. Unfortunately, his ax fell before mine. Ouch, that hurt!

It still hurts my pride and ego. My firing was supposed to remain a secret between my employer and myself. We agreed — myself for reasons of pride and him for fear of wrongful dismissal suits and to avoid the possibility of paying unemployment compensation — that the public would be told I quit.

I still have to smile when I think of him saying to me, "You know if we say you quit you won't be eligible for unemployment." Ha, what a sweetheart turkey he was. Did he think I was going to pay all my bills as well as the mortgage on my home with unemployment compensation?

As you can see, getting fired still rankles me. It's something I have to work harder at letting go of. The best revenge is success. There is life after and I had to get on with it.

A funny thing happened. In the following six months I earned more money than I ever made in a full year working for my former employer. In the following year my income more than tripled. There is life after getting canned and it can be a lot better than the life before.

No, I don't advocate getting fired as a way to a new career and higher earnings. What I do say is that the universe unfolds as it should. In the words of Forest Gump, "Life is like a box of chocolates, you never know what you're gonna get." Just be sure you take a bite.

Twenty-Nine

The Best Thing About Getting Down Is The Way Back Up

The journey is meant to be a trip, not a fall.

I am reminded of the lyrics of an old song, "The best part of breaking up is when we're making up." I can't think of a lot of good in feeling low, being in mental pain — those times in our lives when our feelings are so low that our emotional ceiling seems to be the floor.

I can, however, think of a lot of good in coming back from those times. As an old saying goes, "You don't know how good you can be until you've got to be that good!" The pain of getting in shape is not much fun, but the results are. Your husband or wife leaves you, for good reasons or not, and the pain is terrible. Somewhere down the line (unless you like pain) you move on, grow from the experience, establish a new relationship and look back on that period as a time of growth, discovery and learning. You might even wipe some imaginary sweat off your forehead and say, "Whew — I didn't know how bad off I was back then until I got to where I am today!"

You got fired and ended up in a fresh, successful career. The young fireball pitcher throws his arm out at an early age. After years of rehabilitation he returns as a crafty veteran with an array of off-speed pitches that allow him to have a long, fruitful career — with pitches he would have never bothered to learn had his powerful arm not deserted him.

In a sales career, we often start out being an answer man with little success. You keep answering all the customers' questions and they keep leaving. Then through observation and trial and error, you learn that having the right answers is good, but asking a client or customer the right question is better.

We can succeed through failure and by allowing ourselves to be students who learn from the results of our actions. We can profit in the long run equally from the results of our failures and our successes. Just don't keep failing the same way. Success and failure are often dictated by the patterned responses we follow in any given situation. Is it time for a change?

The catalyst might be something I've written here. More likely it's something that has happened in your own life. It's not who turns the light on that counts, just that it gets switched on somewhere, somehow, sometime, the sooner the better. If it is on, but flickering, turn up the juice or go for a higher wattage. We have the ability to be mental electricians.

Why come so far to stay in the same place? Life is a journey. Of that there is no doubt. There are things in all of our lives that trap us on dead-end avenues or circular highways. I have a bunch of streets named after some of the major issues in my life: Heartbreak Highway, Idiot Avenue, Bumblers Boulevard, Dummy Drive, to name a few. We all do. They are our own private property.

What I have discovered in my life is that along with my dead-end avenues of frustration, I have a far greater number of mental highways to satisfaction. In making others feel good, it automatically makes you better, stronger and more whole. Compliment people, thank people, put a grin on their face and it's a given that there will be a grin on yours. Give something away — money, time, energy, good deeds, good thoughts — and it seems inevitable that the universe somehow, some way, someday will pay you back. Like Jimmy Durante sang, "When you're smiling, the whole world smiles with you."

A good day's work, honest and hard, is a quiet satisfaction that is tough to beat. Sharing the positive, whipping the negative, is the ultimate accomplishment in the workplace. Times of quiet reflection on a job well done can be a peak moment of satisfaction.

Look at a map. The alleys don't show. Build highways of growth, success and appreciation. We are not cogs in a machine, but rather the driving gears of our own lives. Live it, love it, fight for it, it is ours to live. Sometimes it's ours to lose. Never forget amid loss in this business we call life: there is always a "found" department. What I've tried to do here is help you find the ability you possess to make your own deal.

Thirty

39 To Go

And in the end
the effort you take
will equal what you make.

Over the years I have heard or read many worthwhile sayings. On the following two pages is a list of the thoughts that have stayed with me. I would like to share them with you. I've also sprinkled some of my own into the mix.

Put the list on a wall, in your wallet or on your desk. Copy it for a friend or co-worker.

This list hangs on the wall in my office as a reminder — through the tough times, the good times and the best of times — Joe's 39.

Joe's 39

1. Write it down.
2. Follow-up.
3. Be patient.
4. What goes around, comes around.
5. Control your ego...(ouch).
6. Do what you say, say what you do.
7. Respect time — yours and everyone else's.
8. Keep your cool.
9. Don't surrender.
10. Whatever is eating at you — let it go.
11. Keep other's secrets a secret.
12. Talk less, listen well. (You have twice as many ears as tongues for a reason.)
13. If you don't know where you're going, then where are you at?
14. Do your best to deal with the decision-maker.
15. Brainstorm with others.
16. Admit when you don't know.
17. Anticipate problems and, if possible, head them off at the pass.
18. Ignoring a problem won't make it go away.
19. Don't whine much.
20. Build a deal like a house...don't take shortcuts.
21. Tell the truth and you won't have to remember what you've said.

22. Get to the point...and get the point.
23. Be honest, not brutal, about value.
24. When selling, leave enough room for the next guy.
25. Don't act like a big shot.
26. Be confident in your ability but modest about your talent.
27. Be consistent...not predictable.
28. Lead by example.
29. Don't let bastards get you down.
30. Do not underestimate people.
31. Be thankful for what you have.
32. Make the present a compass for your future.
33. Appreciate what is coming in; don't dwell on what is lost.
34. You're a professional — so behave like one.
35. Worry is the interest paid on things that never happen.
36. Don't blow tomorrow's long-term business romance for today's fling.
37. It's better to be nice.
38. A satisfied customer tells five people...a dissatisfied customer tells five hundred. Make them happy.
39. Relax. God is in charge.

A cheeseburger, fries, and 39 to go.

Bibliography

Gibran, Kahlil. *The Prophet.* Alfred A. Knopf, Inc., 1923.

Hill, Napoleon. *Think And Grow Rich.* Fawcett Crest, 1960.

Mandino, Og. *The Greatest Salesman In The World.* Mann Books, 1968.

McCormack, Mark H. *What They Don't Teach You At Harvard Business School.* Bantam, 1984.

Peale, Norman Vincent. *The Power of Positive Thinking.* Fawcett, 1952.

Peck, M. Scott, M.D. *The Road Less Traveled.* Touchstone/Simon & Schuster, 1978.

Ringer, Robert. *Winning Through Intimidation.* Los Angeles Book/Distributed by Funk & Watnalls, 1973.

Warren, Arnie. *The Great Connection.* Pallium Books, 1997.

Ziglar, Zig. *See You At The Top.* Nightingale Conant, 1985.

Index